More praise for *Harnessing America's Wasted Talent: A New Ecology of Learning*

"Love it or not, you've got to read this book. And, not to worry; it's an easy read—Peter Smith's smooth, comfortable writing style makes it easy and enjoyable to get the point. What I most love about the book is Smith's setting of the vision for 'a new ecology of learning' for American higher education, in which the learner controls her learning, not the institution. He envisions a future in which all learning, whether acquired through formal educational formats or otherwise, is assessed validly and then accepted for what it is worth. He sees institutions of higher education, old and new, as central to this learning, but not as the exclusive purveyors of recognized knowledge. His vision is provocative but very realistic."—David Longanecker, former Assistant Secretary for Higher Education and president, Western Interstate Commission for Higher Education

"Smith makes a compelling case for a new ecology of learning, one that is sure to change dramatically the popular conception of higher education as we know it today. His ideas and arguments are thoughtfully presented and make a compelling case for expanding conventional wisdom about how a 'higher education' should be obtained. It squares perfectly with the need to provide individuals with new options for acquiring and documenting knowledge and skills that they will need for productive and happy lives in a world economy that increasingly depends on and rewards both."—Richard Ferguson, chief executive officer, ACT

"This book is thought-provoking and important reading for business, education, and government leaders who believe that we can and must do a better job of developing talent in the United States."—William D. Green, chairman and CEO, Accenture, and chairman, Education, Innovation and Workforce Initiative, Business Roundtable

"In vintage Peter Smith fashion, this new book sweeps across the landscape of higher education's realities in the new, technology-driven American economy, reminding us again of those working adults who have been left behind by the way the current system is organized, funded, and managed. He graphically describes the consequences of failing to educate the bottom two-thirds of our society and convincingly calls for recognizing and assessing learning that people have gained in work, military life, corporate training, and community service as one way to accelerate the progress of working people toward completion of postsecondary education."—Pamela Tate, president and CEO, Council for Adult and Experiential Learning

"Although he writes for a U.S. audience, Peter Smith rings alarm bells for educators in other countries who are busy copying the American higher education system. In a racy, polemical style, he argues that U.S. institutions are the victims of their own previous success and are now incapable of making the changes necessary to serve the many intelligent and committed people who are repelled by current academic practices. Drawing on his own experience of heading innovative institutions at both the college and university level, he outlines a new educational ecology that will take advantage of the growing abundance of learning materials and the opportunities offered by evolving technology to offer personalized education to match the aspirations of millions of frustrated individuals."—Sir John Daniel, president and CEO, Commonwealth of Learning

"*Harnessing America's Wasted Talent* is optimistic about human potential, passionate about educational opportunity, and provocative in its analysis and recommendations. Serious educators and policymakers should read and debate these ideas."—Paul E. Lingenfelter, president, State Higher Education Executive Officers

"Peter Smith provides a compelling statement about the millions of Americans whose skills and contributions are not readily measured by the meritocracy and rigid structures that mark so much of American postsecondary education. His focus on talent—and talent loss—harkens back to identical concerns articulated in a series of national commission reports that began with the historic 1947 Truman Commission Report, *Higher Education for American Democracy*. Although the institutional profile and student population of American higher education has changed dramatically since 1947, Smith reminds us that talent development—and talent loss—remains a continuing concern that has significant consequences for individuals and for the commonwealth."—Kenneth C. Green, founding director, Campus Computing Project

"Peter Smith makes a compelling case for recognizing—and harnessing—the talent of the many Americans who have fallen through the cracks of our country's educational system. This book offers a cohesive road map for institutions to help more individuals find success in today's knowledge-driven economy."—Charles B. Reed, chancellor, California State University

Harnessing America's Wasted Talent

A New Ecology of Learning

Peter Smith

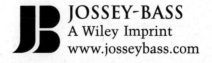

JOSSEY-BASS
A Wiley Imprint
www.josseybass.com

Published by Jossey-Bass
A Wiley Imprint
989 Market Street, San Francisco, CA 94103-1741—www.josseybass.com

Readers should be aware that Internet Web sites offered as citations and/or sources for
further information may have changed or disappeared between the time this was written
and when it is read.

Limit of Liability/Disclaimer of Warranty: While the publisher and author have used
their best efforts in preparing this book, they make no representations or warranties with
respect to the accuracy or completeness of the contents of this book and specifically
disclaim any implied warranties of merchantability or fitness for a particular purpose. No
warranty may be created or extended by sales representatives or written sales materials.
The advice and strategies contained herein may not be suitable for your situation. You
should consult with a professional where appropriate. Neither the publisher nor author
shall be liable for any loss of profit or any other commercial damages, including but not
limited to special, incidental, consequential, or other damages.

Jossey-Bass books and products are available through most bookstores. To contact Jossey-
Bass directly call our Customer Care Department within the U.S. at 800-956-7739,
outside the U.S. at 317-572-3986, or fax 317-572-4002.

Jossey-Bass also publishes its books in a variety of electronic formats. Some content that
appears in print may not be available in electronic books.

Library of Congress Cataloging-in-Publication Data

Smith, Peter, 1945-
  Harnessing America's wasted talent : a new ecology of learning / Peter Smith. – 1st ed.
      p. cm. – (The Jossey-Bass higher and adult education series)
  Includes bibliographical references and index.
  ISBN 978-0-470-53807-4 (cloth)
  1. Educational technology.   2. Education, Higher–Effect of technological
    innovations on.   3. Academic achievement.   I. Title.
  LB1028.3.S59 2010
  378.73–dc22

                                    2009047072

Printed in the United States of America
FIRST EDITION
HB Printing   10 9 8 7 6 5 4 3 2 1

The Jossey-Bass
Higher and Adult Education Series

Contents

Preface

My career has been a continuing personal and professional journey of discovery about adult learning in America. Springing from an instinctive trust in the power and value of experiential learning, grounded in extraordinary learning experiences at the Colorado Outward Bound School and the National Outdoor Leadership School in the 1960s, this journey has proceeded for over forty years. *Harnessing America's Wasted Talent: A New Ecology of Learning* is my best effort to capture and understand the core of my learning during the most recent stage of that journey. In it, I present the synthesized philosophical and operating view that has emerged as a result.

Personal learning is the sum total of all the learning you do, formal and informal, from your perspective. Throughout my career, I have read studies and stories about the power of personal learning. I have tried to understand the different ways that people learn. I have helped design two colleges which create learning environments that support the natural ways people learn. And, through it all, I have worried increasingly about our established colleges' apparent cultural indifference to many types and styles of learning, as well as much of learning's substance.

Human talent is one of America's most important natural resources. And personal learning creates, deepens, and refreshes human talent throughout life. Personal learning is the way that people renew and refresh themselves. We have entered an age in which maximizing human talent is a critical component of human resource, economic, and public education policy. As a result, this vital renewable resource—personal learning—and the talent it nourishes in millions of people can no longer be treated as a sideshow to the main event of higher education.

I have been a personal learner all my life. So have you. Personal learning is the knowledge you gain from your life experiences, including schooling and other courses you take. It includes actual skills and abilities that are marketable, as well as the values, attitudes, perceptions, and understandings that you develop through reflection and introspection. John Dewey examined the relationship between life experiences and personal learning in his book, *Democracy and Education:* "Every experience enacted and undergone modifies the one who acts and undergoes. ... We often see persons ... who have the precious gift of ability to learn from the experiences they have."

Not only do we learn continuously but also our brains are always sorting and sifting through the things that we have learned. Recent research on the human brain suggests that your frontal lobe is more than an equal partner with the rest of the brain. Indeed, it is an orchestrator, refereeing multiple conversations and inquiries behind the scenes while you are doing something else, like sleeping. Imagine it! Your brain is always sorting; sifting; and, well, thinking—looking for answers to questions that matter to you. That explains, possibly, why every now and then we have an "aha!" moment, a realization that comes out of nowhere in an area where we have significant experience and knowledge.

During the last forty years, I have had a series of such moments, each of which has deepened and informed my understanding of learning and the interplay between personal learning, schooling, and work. In each case, it was as if pieces of a puzzle, which had been in front of me so long that I had stopped really looking at them, suddenly took on form and shape. But the "answers" I got weren't solutions. They were guides that cumulatively drove me through fundamental changes in understanding and perception to a new plateau of comprehension, at which I understood and saw things in a new light. There have been three such moments in my life so far.

The Value of Learning Outside of College

The first such change occurred in the early 1970s, when I came to understand that educators routinely ignore the valuable learning that happens outside of colleges. As the founding president of a fledgling new college, the Community College of Vermont, I worked with a gifted team of people to bring postsecondary education to working and poor Vermonters. The experience contained several events that drove my own learning and perception to previously unexplored territory.

As I met with our students, mostly poor and working adults in Vermont, they asked me persistently and urgently why they couldn't get "advanced placement" for things they already knew. Many had been in Head Start training courses offered by local colleges. Would that experience, or their experience working in a Head Start center, count toward a degree?

So I confronted this major issue: why is learning done away from a formal curriculum of little or no value, even if it is sufficiently sophisticated to qualify for credit toward a degree? I have never found a good educational answer to that question. In fact, we lose the value of powerful and effective learning every day because we treat school as the only place where important learning happens. As the opportunity to learn outside of traditional structures has mushroomed in the last thirty years, this academic conceit has evolved into an expensive and scandalous barrier to opportunity.

This experience resulted in my first "aha!" moment. Responding to my new perspective, I wrote *Your Hidden Credentials: The Value of Learning Outside of College* (Smith, 1986). It described the relationship between personal learning outside of a formal school setting, its assessment and validation, and personal development.

What I could not know at the time was that *Your Hidden Credentials* was the beginning of a rich and extended personal learning odyssey for me. Like a telescope, my perspective and knowledge would extend again and then again over the next twenty-five years, allowing me to see things I hadn't seen before and to develop new understandings about learning. Each revelation nourished another, fueling my desire to more fully understand learning in the twenty-first century.

The Law of Thirds

The second stage of this progression was my coming to understand that the way we organize and run colleges and schools, the way we actually educate students, often frustrates learners and inhibits their learning, slowing them down or even depriving them of the benefits of a more formal education. I have come to believe that, in far too many cases, the model we use, not the learners' capacity, is the reason why so many people decide not to continue their education at all, whereas others become statistics in American higher education's high failure rate.

In 2003, deeply troubled by a continuing mind-set of complacency in higher education that consistently shifted the responsibility for learner failure in every direction other than toward colleges themselves, I began research on *The Quiet Crisis: How Higher Education is Failing America* (Smith, 2004). My inquiry included the investigation of a long-held suspicion that our school completion rates were nowhere near as high as the statistics suggested, stemming from an experience I had much earlier in my professional life.

In 1969, I started a learning center for high school dropouts in Montpelier, Vermont. As part of the research for it, I looked at the recent high school completion rates, trying to track when and at what levels students were leaving school. Although the kids were visible on the streets, specific data about dropouts was virtually impossible to find. I was able, however, to identify a significant decline in the general student population between the ninth grade and graduation. But when I questioned people in the school district and the State Department of Education about it, their response was, "Those children moved away." When I asked where they had moved, however, there was no good answer. They had moved away all right, away from school.

As I worked on the manuscript for *The Quiet Crisis*, I came face-to-face with the actual numbers behind the failure rate in America's schools and colleges for the first time. And they confirmed my suspicion that many more people were leaking out of our education system than official reports suggested.

After ten years, roughly one-third of all American ninth graders have not graduated from high school, whereas one-third have graduated but not gone on to college. So, by age twenty-three, 66 percent of all young adults have either no high school diploma or no college experience. The final one-third get a shot at college, with about 60 percent of them attaining at least an associate's degree. All in all, less than 20 percent of all ninth graders have at least an associate's degree within ten years (Mortenson, 2002).

I call this the "Law of Thirds." Put another way, by the time young adults reach the workforce, one-third of them have had the bright flame of their potential crushed during their high school years, while another one-third have survived, although they didn't thrive. The final third, our "success" story, form the core of the workforce and citizen force with which we will face the twenty-first century and its requirements for global economic and political leadership.

The Quiet Crisis called on American higher education to reform. It proposed making room for the millions of people who are currently caught on the far side of the opportunity gap, looking vainly for a way across.

College 3.0

As I spoke with people who read *The Quiet Crisis* and heard their stories, however, I developed a nagging worry that the reform I was calling for could not happen, that higher education as it is organized simply couldn't meet adult learners' needs. This doubt, fed by new research and developing trends, caused my thinking to migrate from higher education reform to a fundamental rethinking of the enterprise. My questioning took a new tack.

- What if failure in school is a function of the educational model's limitations, not the learners'?

- What if people who are capable learners are, in fact, failing for reasons beyond their control?

- What if these marginalized learners share a set of characteristics, beyond race, gender, or economic standing, that we haven't considered before?

- What if, along with the well-documented penalties that come with different cultural and racial histories, gender bias, and poverty, schools and schools' curricula are "unfriendly" for many learners, ignoring their personal capacities to learn and the valuable learning that they achieved in other settings?

We will never forget Einstein. But few of us remember that he was ticketed for expulsion from school at age twelve as unruly and unable to learn.

If, in fact, many people are more capable in real life than schools are able to recognize, then it stands to reason that more adaptive and responsive schools would solve the problem. But this has not happened. Despite enormous effort and attention since the mid 1970s, only marginal gains in college success rates have followed the huge gains of the 1960s and 1970s. We are operating with a "success ceiling," defined by the Law of Thirds, that has been frustrating success rates for several decades. The ability of our system to succeed with more than one-third of its students is under serious question.

Armed with this perspective, I began to look at the collegiate model and several of its core traditional practices in an attempt to understand why so much natural intelligence and learning achievement is routinely stifled and undervalued in America. As part of this inquiry, I also began to consider the possible impact of the Law of Diminishing Returns on our dominant educational model. Our colleges and universities are the envy of many. They have admirable qualities that are undeniable. But they also have limitations that contribute to the diminishing returns we have experienced over the last twenty years. It is ironic. We have a successful model for higher education, but that success comes with a huge, hidden cost: we exclude millions of capable people, frustrating their talent and ignoring their learning.

Our inability as a society to generate better school performance may have as much to do with the model we are using as any other factor. Every model has built-in limitations. And this educational model, organized around place, residential expertise, and time, has been experiencing limitations in its ability to succeed with an increasing proportion of students for the last thirty years.

Is it possible that we need to extend our vision and move beyond improvement in the existing system to an additional, new design of our approaches to teaching and learning? I believe it is. And, in fact, the tools to do so already exist. Even as we have failed to improve college graduation rates over the last thirty years, our universities and entrepreneurs have successfully invented the knowledge and the technology that can write "finished" to this subculture of failure in American education.

Gradually, I have gained two new understandings. First, we cannot win the education battle that confronts us simply by asking colleges and universities to change. Second, our capacity to support, encourage, and recognize learning has not only grown dramatically in the last twenty years, it has also been transformed by a new ecology of learning.

With these things in mind, I have written *Harnessing America's Wasted Talent*. It embraces the learner and learning, reexamines the causes and future consequences of academic failure, and rethinks how to create more chances for success in higher education in the years ahead.

Drawing on research, trend analysis, professional experience, and stories of personal learning in America, *Harnessing America's Wasted Talent* describes how the policies and practices of our dominant college model actually "dumb" some adults down or push them aside entirely when it comes to education after high school. The outrageous truth is that millions of perfectly capable and intelligent people with the ability to learn are kept away from higher education's table of opportunity.

As I develop the case explaining the need for and the inevitability of profound change in the design lying behind higher education, my critique of our current system may seem unduly harsh, or possibly contradictory at some points. Let me clarify in broad strokes my perspective on our current system and the problems we face as a country, ideally reducing such confusion.

Generally, the traditional model of higher education has been successful in educating those students who graduate from high school and go on to college: the "first third" of our high school students. Of the remaining two-thirds, half do not graduate from high school, whereas half graduate but never attempt college-level work. With this profile of the challenge before us, I am constructing the response to it in *Harnessing America's Wasted Talent* as follows.

- Our traditional institutions of higher education must continue to focus primarily on the "first" third. They need to become more successful with a student population that includes growing numbers of low-income, black, and Hispanic students. As we know, we have not served these and some other populations as successfully as we will need to in the future. So, traditional higher education institutions need to focus their reform on improving academic success—qualitatively and quantitatively—with these students. This critique is consistent with the issues raised in *The Quiet Crisis*, and I stand by it today.

- Our traditional model of higher education is not organized and structured to meet the education and workforce training needs of the "middle third": those who have a high school diploma but no college experience. My new design proposals, and the critique that accompanies them, are focused on succeeding with that middle third. They are based on two concepts. First, the new designs must avoid the weaknesses of the current model and focus on meeting the needs of the learners (including the current workforce) and the workplace, while anticipating the need to manage learning throughout life. Second, the new designs will have to embrace emerging knowledge about learning and technological capacities. In so doing, they must be free to organize in ways that are compatible with the strengths and needs of the society around them.

- Elementary and secondary school reform still has a long, steep hill to climb. While strengthening the educational achievement of the top two-thirds of their student population, our K–12 schools need to dramatically reduce the size of the "final third": those who do not graduate or receive a high school diploma. So, our precollege system has its work cut out for it. What I have not done, however, is to push the blame for the problem onto them. If we understand that each sector—K–12, traditional postsecondary, and a new sector encouraged by the new ecology of learning— has a crucial role to play, our chances for success at all levels will improve dramatically.

I focus on higher education and adult lifelong learning in *Harnessing America's Wasted Talent* because it is where my experience and knowledge lie. I believe, however, that the concepts I present and the points I make regarding findings and proposed changes have value for elementary and secondary education as well as traditional higher education. My focus is on reframing the situation—identifying hard truths and describing new possibilities—to stimulate better understanding and new learning. My goal is to make the case for an entirely new dimension in American college, university, and workforce education.

Harnessing America's Wasted Talent will present a new frame of reference coupled with research and experience that support a dramatically different view of the causes and the consequences of college failure, as well as the changes needed to improve learning in the twenty-first century. In far too many cases, failure is a result of the way colleges operate, their tradition and history. It is, in many cases, not indicative of the learner's capacity to learn. This new frame of reference includes solutions that are on the horizon. New ways to deliver, support, and assess learning are developing, which, taken collectively, offer new ways to organize teaching and learning.

Part One of this book, "The Law of Thirds," takes on the issue of the workforce and learning in America, the price of failure in the future, and the reasons why our dominant model for teaching and learning is "maxed out."

Part Two, "Dangerous Conceits," builds on the gaps identified in Part One. It illustrates in greater detail the reasons why higher education, as it is currently organized, will not be able to respond to the challenges facing America, and it turns up the heat on three academic conventions that frustrate the needs and potential of America's adult learners.

"Dangerous Conceits" illustrates that higher education's traditional operational model, although successful for many students, has severe limitations. It can frustrate the best interests, talents, and learning of many adult learners, while ignoring their capacity. Earlier in my career, these practices, and others like them, were rationalized as "the way things are," minor conceits granted to elitist institutions. Today, however, if they are allowed to dominate or stymie expanded learning opportunities, they constitute a clear and present danger to the country's economic, social, and civic future.

Part Three, "From Access to Success: A New Ecology of Learning," has a very basic premise. Entirely new forms of self-reinforcing approaches to high-quality learning are within our reach. We now have the tools and the knowledge to move from promising access to taking responsibility for the success of millions of learners currently languishing outside our system.

The evolution of information technology is valuable far beyond its impact on access. Often seen as an interesting new possibility with significant new expenses, the revolutionary reality of information technology for learning is largely ignored in practice, because its potential value in educating these new learners lies *outside* of the traditional college model and practices.

The emergence of ubiquitous and powerful technologies supplies the tools to transform the orthodox teaching and learning value proposition. They can bring millions who currently live on the margins of American higher education to the mainstream of opportunity. Although still in their infancy, these developments portend a time when content no longer will be the distinguishing characteristic of most colleges. Content will become common, yielding to personalization, support of the learners, and validation of the accomplished learning as the distinguishing quality factors in twenty-first century higher education.

And, in a world in which there will be a chronic shortage of trained teachers as far as the eye can see, thanks to competing careers, poor working conditions, and other obstacles, technology holds the key to learning for millions of students. Even if there are not enough qualified teachers for every twenty students, the opportunities to teach these students anyway, whether they are in Lincoln, Los Angeles, or Lagos, are many, if we see them and use them.

America is poised for a giant step forward in our understanding of how we can legitimately support high-level learning for millions of underserved people, eventually leading to a certificate or degree. In facing this challenge, we know that we have a rich tradition of reinvention, first noted by de Tocqueville in the mid-nineteenth century.

Indeed, protecting the old value proposition while creating a new one is as American as apple pie. The Morrill Land Grant Act and the community college movement exemplify this tradition. They are uniquely American, operating as critical redefinitions of the campus model when they were implemented. And the GI Bill, Pell Grants, and Stafford Loan Program similarly extended the financial resources to let new populations afford a college experience.

This time, however, the pressures and the opportunities call for a change in kind, for new designs. They allow us to create new models that extend and reframe the pattern of higher education that has served us so well for so long. We must act with the knowledge that standing still is losing ground. Without change, there will be little gain.

There are many people who know more, in depth, about many of the things I am treating in *Harnessing America's Wasted Talent*. My intention is not to duplicate or parallel their work. Rather, it is to look across the landscape, connecting several bodies of knowledge and reframing the discussion of what we need and what is possible. I conclude with a new interpretation of where we are right now, why, and what we need to do to achieve the next giant step of improvement for American higher education.

As I have worked, my general indebtedness to several people and institutions has become clear because they have influenced my thinking and development profoundly over the years. First, the innovative institutions at which I have had the privilege of working: the Community College of Vermont; Norwich University; George Washington University; and California State University, Monterey Bay. These experiences have powerfully informed my thinking. When I refer to them in the book, I do so because I lived them, I know them, I understand them, and I believe in them.

Second, the last part of the book, "From Access to Success," has been informed by the professional experiences I have had in the last five years: as a member of the MIT/OpenCourseWare advisory board, as assistant director general for education at UNESCO, and most recently as senior vice president for academic strategy and development at Kaplan Higher Education. Through these experiences, I have had a front-row seat and an immersion experience in the Open Education Resource movement and the technological revolution's impact on learning and education.

Third, I have drawn heavily throughout this effort on the writing, thinking, and work that have been done over the last several years by three people: Bob Jones, Allen Tough, and David Moldoff. Although they don't know one another, their contributions have informed my thinking in immeasurable ways.

- Jones's tremendous insights into workforce trends, based on his years at the United States Department of Labor, where he served as deputy secretary, underpin the workforce theme that you will find throughout the book.

- Tough's seminal work, *The Adult's Learning Projects* (1971), initially defined and typified informal learning.

- Moldoff, whose brilliant conception of the Academic GPS (Guidance, Planning, Success) and the systems and software that lie behind it, along with his company, AcademyOne, represent the coming explosion in thoughtful services that will transform learners' lives.

They have my gratitude for their contributions to higher education. They represent the best that we have and can be.

Finally, as I have written, I have drawn some material from both of my earlier books, including some interview material. In those cases, the names of the subjects have been changed.

I hope *Harnessing America's Wasted Talent* pulls all of us—learners, teachers, business leaders, workers—out of our respective foxholes just a little bit, suggesting a more systemic way of, and a cultural imperative for, valuing what we have in higher education while making space for the dramatic changes we need.

Acknowledgments

In addition to the several institutions and individuals that I cite in the text, there are several organizations that have contributed mightily to the policy debate in higher education over the last two decades. Without their data coupled with thoughtful persistence, the higher education world today would be far less friendly to marginalized learners. These organizations include

- The National Center for Higher Education Management Systems (NCHEMS)
- The Council for Adult and Experiential Learning (CAEL)
- The Western Interstate Commission on Higher Education (WICHE)
- The State Higher Education Executive Officers (SHEEO)
- The National Center for Higher Education Policy (NCHEP), and
- The Institute for Higher Education Policy (IHEP).

They represent the finest that civil society can do to continually press for necessary, responsible change. Their contributions to higher education policy over time have greatly leavened my understanding of the challenges and opportunities that we face.

To Letitia Chambers,
a woman of many talents—
for business, public policy, education, and the arts—
whose great love, thoughtful advice, insightful editing,
and collaboration helped immeasurably
in making this book what it has become.

About the Author

Peter Smith's career spans four decades of innovation and leadership in higher education. Currently serving as senior vice president for academic strategies and development for Kaplan Higher Education (KHE), he has also served as assistant director general for education of the United Nations Educational, Scientific, and Cultural Organization (UNESCO) in Paris and as the founding president at both California State University, Monterey Bay (1994–2005), and the Community College of Vermont (1971–1978). He holds the position of president emeritus at both institutions.

Dr. Smith also served as vice president for development at Norwich University (1986–1988) and as dean of the Graduate School of Education and Human Development for George Washington University (1991–1995).

Dr. Smith is the author of the critically acclaimed *The Quiet Crisis: How Higher Education Is Failing America* (2004), which won the Frandson Award for Literature in the Field of Continuing Higher Education. His many distinctions and awards include *Esquire* magazine's Best of the New Generation (1984) and *Change* magazine's Outstanding Educators in the United States Under Age Forty (1978), and he was the corecipient of the National Council of Community Service and Continuing Education "Man of the Year" award with Senator Walter Mondale (1976).

He has served as chair of the board of directors of the Fund for the Improvement of Post Secondary Education, as well as on the boards of the Council for the Assessment of Experiential Learning, the National Center for Higher Educational Management Systems, the Education Commission of the States, the Carnegie Forum on Education and the Economy, and the Wingspread Group on Higher Education. In 1991, Smith served as a senior fellow at the American Council on Education.

A native of Vermont, Smith served there as a state senator, as lieutenant governor, and as a member of the United States Congress.

Dr. Smith holds an Ed.D. in Administration Planning and Social Policy and an M.A. in Teaching from Harvard University. He received his B.A. in American History, magna cum laude, from Princeton University.

Harnessing America's Wasted Talent

Part I

The Law of Thirds

American higher education is operating under a dangerous assumption: that we have always "met the challenge" and that, if we will only work hard, we can meet whatever challenges lie ahead. This section presents three reasons why that assumption has become dangerous, threatening our position as a world economic, civic, and intellectual leader.

The first chapter, "Wasted Talent," describes the extent to which we actually overlook the extraordinary talent that many people have. It profiles the extent of the challenge we face in harnessing that talent and the costs of failing to do so, arguing that educational success for many people and our future economic health are inextricably connected. It also discusses the implications of failure in terms of frustrated opportunity in America, loss of productivity and global position, and lower earnings and tax contributions.

Chapter Two, "Maxed Out: Why Colleges Can't Meet This Challenge," develops the case that our "system" of higher education has little prospect of meeting the new educational challenges facing us. While arguing in favor of their continued vitality and central importance, it also suggests that "what got us where we are won't get us where we need to go."

Although the Law of Thirds is not intentional, it does signify the upper limit of our traditional colleges' and universities' ability to serve learners successfully. The chapter discusses some of the limitations in the American model of higher education. They include

- a lack of trained faculty,
- academic tradition and culture,
- an exclusive approach to teaching that frustrates many learners, and
- the politics of scarcity that define a campus's structure.

Chapter Three, "The Paradox of Personal Learning," describes the extraordinary gap between how people learn and what they know, on the one hand, and how the society harnesses that learning, on the other. Several vignettes personalize the rich, varied, and diverse ways that people learn. Along with revealing individuals' excitement about "personal learning," the stories describe the scorn for, fear of, and anger at colleges and workplaces that many people feel. Buttressed by these vignettes, the chapter lays the groundwork for the proposition that personal learning is continuous; important; valuable; complex; and, paradoxically, largely ignored. It symbolizes the wasted talent that we need to harness.

1

Wasted Talent

I am an experienced older American worker. I have gained streams of workplace experience that were obtained without a formal education. ... [My life] situation forced me to take this path. Now, to get the same job I've held for so many years, I need a degree. I can't change my past, but what about me now? ... I shouldn't be ruled out. People like myself hold wells of workplace experience that are still useful and productive and can help with this employment situation. (Faith, blog entry, rethinkinghighereducation.com, 2008)

Faith is just one of millions of people who have been left in the dust by an approach to education and learning that says, "Classroom first, and nothing else matters." As we will see, there are tens of millions of adults in the workforce who have not been able to achieve recognition for their learning or their capacities at the postsecondary level. Each person's case, taken individually, may seem like a sad song; even, perhaps, a little whiney. But millions of such cases, taken together, create a rising chorus of pain and waste, which crescendos into a weaker social and civic life and a declining ability to compete in the global economy.

For the first time in our history, we are creating more jobs requiring high skills and talent than we are educating people to fill them. We cannot afford to ignore the talent of people like Faith any longer. Wasting talent has transitioned away from being largely a moral issue to becoming a national security issue.

As a result, we stand at a crossroads in American history. For more than two hundred years, the American example has rested on our people: how we treated each other; how we behaved in a democratic republic; and what we did with our hands, our courage, and our ingenuity. Imagine an American future that is compromised socially, civically, and economically, at home and around the world, because, just when we needed it the most, we refused to recognize the talent that we have. And imagine that, with that refusal, we had forfeited our national capacity to think, invent, and change—our ability to continue our leadership in a rapidly changing global marketplace.

Wasted talent is putting our leadership position in the world at risk. For the first time in a century, some people are beginning to wonder whether the American example will continue to inform and illuminate the dark corners of human existence.

In engineering there is a phrase that describes the angle at which any substance will settle if you put it against a vertical surface. Engineers initially used it to determine when it was safe to go near huge amounts of slag or excavated material, heaped against the side of a canyon wall. Wallace Stegner used this term as the title of his extraordinary book, *Angle of Repose* (1971). In the book, Stegner was referring to human relationships, describing how they reach an "angle of repose" over time, settling to the point where there is no more significant movement. This marvelous, if disturbing, metaphor suggests a final resting place for people, relationships, countries, and civilizations. In it, each entity has its own angle of repose—the point at which the dynamism ceases and the future is largely stable, fixed, and understood.

I am urgently concerned that America's system of higher education has reached its own angle of repose. As I analyze America's wasted talent and its impact on our future, the questions come at me. Is our social, civic, and economic future fixed and determined by the current capacity and quality of our educational institutions? Are there other ways to educate millions of people who are currently poorly served by the existing system?

This angle of repose cuts two ways. First, it characterizes the diminishing capacity of our system to educate more people well. Second, it describes the impact of that failure on the larger society. We are denying millions of people a seat at the table of economic opportunity and the personal satisfaction that comes with it. And we are denying American competitiveness and prosperity the power boost that harnessing our wasted talent would give it.

When I grew up in Vermont, we understood that the salt used to clear the roads in the winter was bad for the cars and the trucks. Even though you couldn't see it happening, the salt accumulated in the undercarriages, eating away at the metal frames and destroying the vehicles.

Just as road salt eats away at the undercarriage of a Vermont pickup truck, wasted talent and the denied opportunity that goes with it corrode the social, civic, and economic undercarriage of our democracy. Invisibly, wasted talent eats away at each person's hope for a better future, the self-respect that comes with pride in personal performance and with the ability to provide for one's family and participate in the life of the community. Wasted talent is not simply an individual's problem, or someone else's problem, it is a national economic and security issue that needs to be addressed.

I approach the urgency I feel about wasted talent with some caution, however. I am not a radical. Raised in a moderate republican family in Vermont, I was encouraged to believe in the value of the democratic process, in America's special place in the world, and in the need for peace and harmony as prerequisites for economic stability and prosperity. Above all, I was encouraged to believe in the institutions of government, including universities, as part of the "sacred secularity" that is American democracy. Voting, I came to understand, is our secular religion, tying us all to the grand vision of a life of opportunity together. In that vision, learning is the key to personal success and crucial to our success as a society.

But, with a nod to caution, we need to sound the alarm. There are numbers that describe the serious situation we face. Sometimes, however, statistics don't sufficiently humanize a crisis, compelling people to pay attention. And of course there is the old skepticism about "Lies, damn lies, and statistics." America, it is said, is always better at responding to a crisis than anticipating one. We like to see the problem before we solve it. Or, as Winston Churchill allegedly put it, "America always comes up with the right solution, but only after trying all other possibilities!"

If we wait on this problem, it will be too late. It will be like waiting until the ninth ward in New Orleans is flooded and gone before we take action, even though we know the consequences of not maintaining the levees on the Mississippi River. Or waiting until a small island nation in the Indian Ocean prepares to disappear before we understand one practical impact of global warming. Or waiting until trillions of dollars simply melt into nothing under the harsh sun of wanton irresponsibility and rapacious greed, throwing people out of work and out of their homes, before we understand that not all financial regulation is bad.

We need to think ahead about the solutions to wasted talent. But sometimes thinking ahead is not what we do best. So, as we prepare to think about the cost of wasted talent in America, let's think first about America's place in the world and the consequences of additional economic weakness and failure.

For the last one hundred years, we have stood as a bastion for many things, including entrepreneurship and free enterprise, liberty and justice, and the enduring power of the separation of church and state under the consent of the governed. Despite our well-recorded struggles with fairness and racism, we have been more welcoming than any other country, becoming home to millions of people from around the world. All of this rests on the foundation of an enduring and representative democracy.

America and the American promise stand at the intersection of two powerful concepts and life forces: liberty and justice. Liberty is the icon of individualism, the inalienable right of the individual to life, liberty, and the pursuit of happiness. It promises that we will be free from the domination of others, free to speak, to practice religion—or not, as we please—to make our own ways.

But liberty is balanced out by justice, a competing and complementary concept. Justice is the concept of the common good, the commitment that people will be treated fairly under the law. We agree that there are legitimate interests of the many over the few, to be moderated and determined by the three branches of government.

These two powerful philosophies ebb and flow in America along the political spectrum, from Adams to Jefferson, from Lincoln to Roosevelt, and from Reagan to Obama—each having a different view. They are sometimes competing philosophies, but they are both embraced by our democratic system.

Some would argue that America's greatness is captured in our institutions of government, the Bill of Rights, the Constitution, or the separation of powers. As revolutionary and historic as these documents and concepts are, however, they are only the skin and bones of democracy. They would mean little without a citizenry willing to believe in them. I believe that the genius of American democracy lies in hope, the promise of opportunity for all, a belief that your children will have a better life than you.

The presence of hope in people's hearts is what makes America great and binds our society together, carrying oxygen to all parts of our civic and social body. And, if the promise of opportunity is the bloodstream of America, then learning and education are the mighty beating heart that makes the blood flow, creating and nurturing our human talent.

The American promise is that there are as many seats at the table of opportunity as there are people who wish to take one. In America, you do not have to wait for someone to die, or push someone off his or her seat to get your opportunity. Here, we say you don't have to stand in line. If you work hard, you can grab the dream and have a seat at the table of opportunity with everyone else.

With this cultural and political dynamism based on opportunity, we stand as a beacon of hope and possibility in a world that is still too much caught by the hierarchies of the past, by ancient divisions that divide people and frustrate their abilities to prosper. And, if recent history has taught us anything, it has taught us that these chaotic forces of dark history are still there, loaded with the latent ability to destroy social, civic, and economic organization. It is important that we endure.

America's emergence as the undisputed world leader occurred in recent history, over the last one hundred years. The low point of this period followed World War I, the decades of the 1920s and 1930s. Trade barriers went up, destroying markets around the world. Cultural isolationism and hierarchy were rampant as people retreated within their personal histories and national borders for comfort. Paradoxically, at the same time, the country also joined others in a futile search for world peace through the naïve "Treaty to End All Wars," Kellogg-Briand.

We all know what happened next: the worst depression in the history of the world, with the resulting rise of the worst demagogues in the history of the world—Hitler, Mussolini, and Stalin. Ultimately, untold millions suffered and died in the worst war in the history of mankind. This is the bitter harvest reaped from a provincial isolationism that infected most aspects of American life during that period. We learned that it does not work to retreat from the world.

Just as surely as we withdrew from the world, however, America rose mightily to the extraordinary challenge of dealing with the consequences of isolationism. America anchored the forces in all theaters of World War II that led to victory. And America also had the foresight and the courage to anticipate the war's successful aftermath with such brilliant programs as the Marshall

Plan and support for creating the United Nations. This was, truly, our finest hour—the high point in the century of American emergence.

Since the century's midpoint, the American promise to the world has been challenged from within and without. Our greatest foreign policy victory was a war with few military battles, the Cold War. The strategy of containment served us well, using the examples of American life and economic democracy to shine as the preferred alternatives to communism and dictatorship. At the same time, our military excursions thereafter—Korea, Vietnam, Iraq—met with increasing resistance and, at best, mixed results.

Over the same period of time, a world diminished in size by modern travel and communications has seen its economic structure and potential increase dramatically. The global economy has erupted, with both significant environmental consequences and the emergence of a super-elite, which has amassed an astonishing percentage of the world's resources, earnings, and assets.

Where does this leave America and the American example? Are we in the early stages of an extended period of stagnation leading to ultimate decline, seeking our angle of repose as has been the story with other empires? Or will we gather our resources and our wits, and reenter the fray in appropriate ways to engage and deepen our leadership of the global saga that is unfolding?

As the assistant director general of education at the United Nations Education, Science, and Cultural Organization (UNESCO), I watched the expenditure of the final goodwill credited to America's account when our soldiers liberated Europe during World War II. Years of growing frustration with our approach to foreign affairs, cultural encroachment, and global economics hardened into a cold hostility toward the government of America. And, among less developed countries, there was a persistent level of suspicious resignation that America and other developed countries would have their way first, with only the crumbs left for the "home" country's indigenous aspirations and plans.

As I returned home from UNESCO, I studied this perspective from the American view. It didn't look much better. Our greatest threat is internal, stemming from a combination of domestic near-sightedness and a complacent arrogance about our role in the rest of the world. Perhaps it is natural to worry about ourselves first. But it is dangerous and counterproductive to believe that the way we do things will ultimately be "best" for the world. Indeed, in some cases, "the way we do things" has reached its limits of effectiveness for us as a country as well.

The structure of our higher education system and our rising tide of wasted talent are worrisome cases in point. We have a system of higher education that is admired by the rest of the world. Other countries are copying it, even partnering with our institutions as a development strategy in some cases. Yet the costs and consequences of wasted talent, to be fully reaped in the future when our failures have compounded, are already accumulating at our feet.

Education and workforce development are domestic issues. But they have global repercussions. Without domestic success in these areas, our economy will be seriously and structurally weakened, prolonging if not driving a continuing global downturn that will have a devastating effect. Getting this issue right, here in America, so that people have a way to achieve the American Dream once again, is also critically important to the welfare of the world.

Shortly before President Obama's inauguration in 2009, I wrote him an open letter on my blog, www.rethinkinghighereducation, about wasted talent. I addressed the letter to the president because it allowed me to organize the critical nature of the education and workforce crises we face in a policy-political framework. I wrote,

Dear President Obama,

You are facing two crises of immense proportion and complexity: in foreign affairs and finance. They are harvested, I believe, from a complacent, arrogant, and outdated assumption about American destiny in the world. I am writing you about a third such crisis, not yet fully shaped. But, like a tsunami, it is beginning to suck our resources out to sea before inundating our shores with further social, civic, and economic pain. It also is incubated by an arrogant complacency fueled by America's historic superiority in higher education.

Let me share some hard truths. Although we have a fine higher education system, it cannot solve this problem for us. Consider the situation we face.

- We are the only developed country in which younger workers are less well educated than older workers.
- Our workforce is aging, retiring, and declining.
- The number of new jobs is growing, with predicted skilled worker shortages of 7 million in 2010 and 21 million in 2020.
- Right now, 85 percent of all new jobs require at least some postsecondary education.
- By 2014, 78 percent of all jobs will require some postsecondary education.

Against this future, we have a system of schooling that currently is losing one-third of all students before high school graduation, with only 18 percent actually proceeding to at least the associate's degree by age 23.

We are missing the workforce education mark we need to hit in 2014 by 50 percent. And all the people available to work in 2014 are already in the education pipeline: high school and college! If, however, we think fixing the pipeline will solve the problem, we are making a dreadful error. The number of people in the pipeline is stagnating, and we already have a surplus of jobs with a deficit of documented talent, making a robust business future unattainable. Once this tsunami hits us, it will be too late to respond effectively.

The solution: We can generate the 7 million more highly skilled workers we need from the adult population that we already have.

There are over 40 million American adults with high school diplomas, some college-level learning, and an enormous amount of learning and experience accumulated in noncollegiate settings. We should acknowledge their unrecognized knowledge and skills and put them to use in the American workplace (Jones, 2009).

To achieve this, direct the Department of Education to commission a Request for Proposal that asks accredited institutions of higher education and other educational entities to propose how they will

- accept certificates recognizing corporate and workplace-based training for academic credit,
- accept military and other recognized education and training for academic credit,
- assess other life experience, using validated procedures, for academic credit,
- recognize all transcripted college learning from accredited colleges for progress toward the degree, and
- put it all on a consolidated, approved transcript, so that the transcript holder can move forward educationally and economically in the workplace.

We know how to do these things right now. The only obstacles are academic tradition, arrogance, and conceit.

Mr. President, please don't fall into the "skill training" trap. We need thinkers who can work and workers who can think. Business Round Table and Chamber of Commerce surveys show that employers want three things, above all else, in their new workforce.

1. Workers who can "self-direct" and adapt
2. Workers with a global perspective
3. Workers who can think critically and write

Harvesting the skills, knowledge, and ability that are already resident in our workers won't take a lot of money. It will, however, take something else, something easy to say and extremely difficult to do: the ability to change how we look at learning, where it happens, and how we value it. Promote that change and we can rejuvenate America's economy from the inside out.

Sincerely,

Peter Smith

The adult learners we will meet in future chapters lie behind these statistics and philosophy. They, and millions of others like them, are out there, living and learning valuable behaviors, skills, and abilities. But they are blocked from having their true potential recognized and from benefiting from that recognition by the success ceiling in American education. As a result, their talent is compromised and wasted.

They are capable people. But they are also casualties, wasted talent reflected in the grim statistics of the Law of Thirds. Alan, a blogger who responded to a piece I wrote, addressed the Law of Thirds and its impact on him.

I am one of the two-thirds without the degree that you mentioned. I have been running my own business for the last ten years. During that time, I have acquired numerous skills and a tremendous amount of knowledge. I am now at a point in my life where I want to move on to the next challenge. Unfortunately, any job listing I come across that I am qualified for in regard to the position, I do not meet the educational requirements. I know in my heart that I have plenty to offer. I also know that a degree will open more doors for me. I have looked into getting credit for my work experience, but the process is cumbersome and lengthy for a working adult with a family. The kind of aggressive innovation that adults like me need involves streamlining that process. Instead of discouraging people like me, embrace us and discover the talent and innovation we can bring to the workforce.

As you consider these stories, you will begin to see the many ways that the success ceiling operates to keep people out.

- Colleges are psychologically remote, holding people away with a reputation as places that are alien to working adults. They have the aura and mystery of the unknown, or forbidden fruit.

- Colleges are experientially remote. They don't recognize the value of learning that happens somewhere else, outside of college. Imagine having your entire life experience—work, personal, and social—nullified by an arbitrary historic practice.

- Colleges are physically remote, requiring a time and time-of-week commitment that simply does not align well with other demands on an adult's life.

- Colleges are academically remote, refusing to honor credits earned at other colleges, in the military, or in corporate training.

- Colleges are financially remote, requiring too much expense and debt to get to the degree.

- Most colleges have enrollment limits, enforced by funding, space, and reputation, making them unavailable to many people.

To the person on the outside looking in, any one of these obstacles is huge. But when taken in combinations, they appear to be evidence that college is for someone else. Millions of good people simply do not have an option. They are defeated by "the way things have always been."

Having lost a fight they never picked, these capable, interesting, accomplished adults are trapped on the far side of the bright line of learning, separated from formal education and the benefits it brings by the success ceiling in American higher education.

This is bad business for them, but it is worse for society.

The Law of Thirds forces a waterfall of talent over the edge of the educational cliff, cascading into the streambed of life below. Wasted talent is a two-edged sword. It is a human and financial tragedy for the individual. These people will earn less and contribute less to the support of the government while, in all likelihood, consuming more government services during their lifetimes. It is a public economic tragedy as well, hollowing out the workforce of the future, leaving it woefully underpopulated and unable to sustain robust economic growth.

Think of it. By the time young adults reach the workforce, one-third of them have had their potential dismissed or ignored during their high school years, whereas another one-third have survived, although they didn't thrive. The final third, our "success" story, form the core of the workforce and citizen force with which we will face the twenty-first century and its requirements for global economic and political leadership.

If tomorrow's projected workforce were an army, it would make Washington's army at Valley Forge seem like a juggernaut. Tactics, daring, and the weather alone won't win this battle, however. Only programs that unlock talent will win the day.

There are four elements in this equation: the current workforce, current and future job creation, necessary preparation, and current capacity in the younger workforce. When you look at each of these elements, and then take them collectively, you can see that if things do not change dramatically, America will not be able to compete as effectively in the global economy over time.

Just as water is sucked out to sea before the tsunami surges in, the lack of adequately prepared workers is the outflow of recognized human talent prior to the economic tsunami about which I warned in my letter to President Obama. Quietly, older workers are disappearing from our workforce. And, just as quietly, we are failing to replace them with workers who have the skills necessary to do the job. When the wave comes ashore, it will be too late. Workers with necessary skills won't exist and the jobs will be gone, lost either overseas or to a low-performing economy. And America and the world will be at risk.

As the data in my letter to President Obama clearly indicates, America is missing the critical education-workforce development mark on all important scales. We will have fewer workers, who are more poorly trained, in a market of growth in jobs that require more higher education and greater sophistication and skill levels. Instead of doubling our number of college graduates by 2020, we are on track to either stand still or improve slightly, missing the mark by millions of people and jobs.

In his speech to Congress in February 2009, President Obama made a direct connection between our failure to educate all our citizens and our economic weakness. He called on all Americans to attain some college experience after earning their high school diplomas. The President recognized that we cannot afford to deny access to higher education and advanced work skills to two-thirds of our population. It is socially, civically, and economically untenable. The Law of Thirds is an algorithm that explains the failure of our schools with these populations. We must break the ceiling imposed on success by the Law of Thirds and stop wasting our native talent, attaining greater levels of educational achievement by many more people. Then, a new algorithm will emerge.

Failure to break through the success ceiling has significant social, civic, and economic consequences for our country. A population that can't provide for itself is a population deprived of the basic American promise: hope for a better future. American learners need the learning they have been denied. And America needs a civic force and workforce ready for the twenty-first century.

The success ceiling has several facets. It can be:

- circumstantial (your life circumstances change);
- psychological (you have been convinced that you are a "loser");
- financial (over a million high school graduates each year do not attend college, although they are qualified);
- qualitative (the curriculum and classrooms are biased against certain types of intelligence and learning styles); or
- quantitative (there are a limited number of spaces for students to occupy, so some are left behind).

But the consequence is always the same: wasted talent.

The success ceiling operates invisibly. There is no count of the fallen, beyond the notoriously understated and unreliable drop-out rate. It is similar to the highway bridge that fell into the river in St. Paul, Minnesota, a few years ago. There had been reports of structural weakness on file for years. But, like wasted talent, the weakness was ignored because it was invisible, until the bridge fell down.

The critical question remains: How will we unlock the talent we have in America? Who will do it?

The first part of the answer to this critical question may sound counterintuitive to some people, given my tone so far in the book.

In order to unlock the talent we have, we need our traditional colleges and universities to keep doing what they are already doing, and to do it better. There are three reasons for this.

- First, they are good at educating many of the students who currently attend and they are getting better every day. In addition, their contributions to research and knowledge development are unparalleled.

- Second, their graduates are the foundation of any long-term solution we develop, the down payment on the future we seek. So, we need their graduates now, more than ever. A jaguar is a beautiful, swift-running animal. Our colleges and universities have honed their capabilities. Let them run.

- The third reason, the subject of the next chapter, is more complex. For all the things it does well, traditional higher education as we currently know it is largely "maxed out." It has reached the point of diminishing returns when it comes to addressing this new challenge and the new learners who come with it. We need a "new breed of cat" to break through the success ceiling in American higher education.

America's higher education history is a proud one. But asking our existing institutions to meet the problems that face our country and our workers today, to take sole responsibility for productively harnessing America's wasted talent, would be a grave error.

Some may think that I am being too extreme in my analysis of this problem. Others may think that I am mischaracterizing the capacity of our current institutions to respond. Our recent experiences, however, suggest otherwise. Throughout my adult life, I have watched these problems, and others, fester without resolution.

In some other areas of former American dominance, outside of education, the chickens are coming home to roost. The American production model, unchecked and embraced by China's billions of people, may well warm the globe and change the life patterns and the economies of additional billions in the process. The American automobile industry, having successfully frustrated mass transportation in the 1950s, is running out of cheap oil and highway inventory. Their model is collapsing, and so are the companies and the communities in which they reside. And some of our banks and other financial institutions have ridden the American model of free enterprise right off the cliff, weakening the country and the world's economy.

In light of these consequences of American arrogance and shortsightedness, consider the impending situation in higher education and workforce development. Our education system is mature, whereas our global competitors' systems are still developing. If we are "maxed out," the system is doing the best it can do. That is its effective "success ceiling," its angle of repose, the limit to its productivity. Faced with the need for dramatic education improvements, our dominant educational model is hamstrung, producing diminishing returns against the growing need.

If this is true, our overseas competitors don't need to beat us in education, they just have to do as well. Even if the developing nations of the world are affected by the Law of Thirds and ultimately stall out at the same success ceiling as America, they will swamp the global marketplace with new, educated entrants before they hit the ceiling. How can we possibly compete with a China, let alone a world, that has not yet achieved our level of success within its own population?

If we don't break through the success ceiling, less-developed countries will swamp us with the sheer numbers of their educated new entrants to the global workforce, as they move toward their one-third plateaus. Their advantage in this competition lies squarely in the fact that they are currently behind us in the development of the dominant model. In a world that is developing rapidly, America is standing still.

America's system of higher education has drawn a bright line between the learning that goes on in a person's life and the learning that occurs in colleges and universities. On one side of the line, we have millions of capable people leading productive lives with little or no recognition of the valuable knowledge they have. On the other side, we find a smaller group, those lucky enough to have found and fit into higher education the way it is organized. Their academic learning and the credentials that certify it give them the inside track to economic and social opportunity.

This bright line contradicts both common sense and the promise of opportunity embedded in the American Dream. It is also bad business for a country that needs all the talent it can get to prosper civically, socially, and economically.

This double standard operates in the workplace as well, where the same system of rewards and credentials fails to recognize personal learning, thus denying mobility.

- A woman returning to paid work after years of raising a family, managing a household, and organizing hundreds of community events finds that there is no way to cash in on the knowledge and skills she has developed over the years.

- Returning soldiers get partial or no recognition for the training and the experience they have accumulated during their service years.

- A senior employee is forced to train her new supervisor for the job she can do but can't have because she doesn't have the required degree.

- Courses and continuing education seminars taken elsewhere are not trusted by the employers.

It is a system that, at its worst, is dominated by an academic marketplace that emphasizes credentials over competence, overlooking the very human resources it is supposed to strengthen.

2

Maxed Out

Why Colleges Can't Meet This Challenge

American higher education is a wonder of the modern world. Stretching from the tip of Macias, Maine, to the Big Island of Hawaii, and from Key West to Nome, it is without parallel in history.

Not only is American higher education expansive, it is diverse. This nation hosts more than four thousand colleges, ranging from two-year to doctoral, public, private, liberal arts, technical, market-driven, religious, and nonsectarian institutions (U.S. Department of Education, 2001). The list is long and the variety amazing.

If you look closely at this wonder of wonders, however, you will be reminded that our system of higher education is not a system at all. It actually resembles a large and diverse cottage industry with many members all making a version of the same product. Some institutions are affiliated with others, some are not. Some have storied histories and global alumni groups; others' names are barely known within their neighborhoods. Although each is considered a postsecondary institution, each has its own unique history, mission, and orientation.

Our higher education "system" is, in fact, a collection of highly autonomous, independent institutions, vigorously resistant to any overarching or outside control. In fact, if we reflect on it just a little, we do not want our colleges and universities to be all the same or do all the same things. This independence of thought and action, this variety, is a great strength. We have developed this system through a national consensus that colleges of great value to the individual learner may also be very different from one another.

Despite this diversity of mission, orientation, and governance, however, the operating structure and assumptions behind how these colleges operate have changed less over the last three hundred years than any other western institution. In fact, as Clark Kerr, the legendary leader of California's higher education system, allegedly observed, when Vatican II removed Latin from the Roman Catholic mass, this observation probably became true. Virtually all of our schools, from nursery schools to postgraduate institutions, reflect an educational model that has been in place since the fourteenth century.

This operational model is based on assumptions and traditions that have long outlived not only their usefulness but also their logic. For example, the idea of a scholar-professor standing in front of students to speak in a lecture format predates the printing press. Our academic calendars are perfectly matched to the needs of an agricultural society now long dead. Although our society needs graduates who are educated to think critically and analytically and apply knowledge in the outside world, most education occurs in a traditional academic environment, far from the streets below. And we still operate on the assumption that all important teaching and learning happens in school classrooms, regardless of their type. All too often, the connection between a typical university curriculum and the actual, lived experiences of today's university students is largely nonexistent.

Within our diversity of institutional form and behind our historic commitment to access, there is a numbing sameness in our assumptions when it comes to teaching and learning. The causes behind the Law of Thirds lie where we actually do higher education, on our campuses, in our classrooms, and in our traditions.

Different colleges recruit different students, serve different audiences, and teach different knowledge, but they do it all through the same basic model: employing scholar-professors, in front of students, isolated from the world, with classes organized into standard blocks of time with a central text or syllabus that will fill a three-credit course with instruction, papers, exams, and grades. The sameness of how we teach from one campus to another is staggering. We are universal in expecting the same thing from our students: that they come as they are and be ready to learn; to absorb the teaching and prove they learned it; and, maybe, to go on to a higher level for more of the same.

Accounting and history, criminal justice and psychology are presented the same way. The wealthiest, most elite university on the east coast subjects its students to largely the same process that will be suffered by the newest recruit at a community college in New Mexico. Although technology has certainly modified many a course presentation, the underlying realities are consistently traditional. The course design continues to treat all students largely the same when it comes to teaching. And the cost of technology is treated as an add-on, not an investment in transformation.

This sameness is as if there were hundreds of restaurants, each claiming to be unique, all serving one dish: white rice. Some might be fried, some might be steamed with saffron. Some might even be part of a fricassee dish. But it's all rice. No matter where you go, which campus you visit, what students you interview, the assumptions behind teaching and learning are unchanged. At Yale and Yakima, backpack-wearing students absorb knowledge from someone wiser, regurgitate the knowledge to the wiser person's satisfaction, receive grades, move on to sit in more classes, absorb knowledge from someone wiser, and so on.

Since the passage of the GI Bill in June 1944, we have built ways for millions of Americans to get into and go to college that are second to none in history. Four years after the close of World War II in 1949 there were 1,851 degree-granting institutions in

America. Today, there are over 4,000. They come in every shape, size, and type, from seminaries to trade schools, from the state universities of the Midwest to Ivy League research centers and football powerhouses.

Those who lived through these years witnessed the phenomenal rise of community colleges and the concurrent expansion of state colleges and universities. We have more than doubled the number of colleges by legislating dollars at the state and federal levels, pouring public funds into coffers also holding private contributions and student payments. And, in a second radical departure from the historic norm, we have subsidized students directly with Pell grants and Stafford loans, giving them the power to choose their colleges for themselves. We have implemented these policies because we hold one collective goal: an affordable, high-quality college education within easy reach of every American.

In some important respects, we have succeeded beyond our fathers' and mothers' wildest dreams. Immediately after World War II, less than 30 percent of high school graduates, the qualified relevant age cohort, enrolled in higher education in the United States. For a comparison, look to the Europe of that time, where an elite higher education system was maintained with fewer than 5 percent of the same group attending postsecondary institutions. By 1960, Europe had increased access to more than 15 percent, whereas the United States was approaching 50 percent of possible qualified students actually seeking entry to college.

This classic model has worked pretty well for America. So, why aren't our colleges and universities, and the model that they employ, the solution to the problems we face now?

First, colleges are difficult organizations to change. And we know that they have gotten even larger and more unwieldy in the last century. In 1920, the average four-year institution had 457 enrolled students, and the average two-year college enrolled 154. By 1980, these numbers had swelled to 4,070 and 3,604, respectively. Today, the numbers are even more exaggerated. And these averages mask the real story about typical institutional size.

Behind the averages, more than half of all college and university students—and nearly half of all professors—inhabit the mere 10 percent of institutions that enroll more than ten thousand students. The actual landscape of institutions has roughly 400 campuses educating 50 percent of the students, with the remaining 3,600 institutions educating the other 50 percent. Institutions of such magnitude carry with them significant inertia that resists change in countless ways.

Even within small institutions, the weight of tradition is leveraged against every appeal for change. The tradition of faculty governance is perhaps the best single example of this reality. It is built on the premise of academic freedom, the important concept dictating that the content and academic process on a campus should be free of external political influence and that faculty should manage their own affairs.

But faculty governance never envisioned a world in which the rate of change off campus was far greater than the rate of change on campus. Nor did it anticipate the ability to analyze how people learn best and integrate that knowledge into the curriculum. And, in a world where books were precious, open educational resources and free content were unimaginable. So, a critical protection from one era is transformed into a potential obstacle to improvement in another. Organizational change comes hard at colleges and universities.

Indeed, colleges and universities are some of the best examples of the phenomenon that Mary Douglas saw in all sorts of institutions: "There are four decisive arguments against organizational change," she wrote. "There is no time. It is unnatural. God prohibits it. And there is no money" (quoted in Keller, 1983). Most of us have experienced many variations on these themes. And we will hear them again every time we propose to revamp established collegiate models and programs to match the realities of a learning-centered age.

The second factor opposing change, however, goes to the heart of actually solving America's problem with wasted talent. Continuing to rely on the traditional model flies directly in the face of what we know about how people learn, the opportunities that technology presents to transform the educational enterprise, and our historic record of educational failure with a rapidly diversifying population. Not only are many traditional policies unfriendly to many learners, but also colleges' classic way of hosting teaching and learning is unfriendly.

The traditional academic model has not harnessed and integrated the extraordinary technological resources we are creating, which have the capacity to transform teaching and learning. And it hasn't made room for the new knowledge being created about the many ways that intelligence works and people learn. In plain terms, it has not, and I believe it cannot, get us where we want to go as a society committed to equal opportunity for all and to sound economic growth based on a fully educated workforce.

Finally, colleges can't control their costs. They are expensive and becoming more expensive, with costs that are outstripping inflation, health care, housing, and buying power. In the study *Measuring Up 2008*, the National Center for Public Policy and Higher Education described a collision course between college costs and the perceived value of a college education. Increasingly, Americans believe that college is more important than ever. They also believe that, for whatever reason, college costs are escalating far beyond their reach, forcing them to choose between intolerable debt burdens or denied access (Lewin, 2008).

These are the feelings of the public as they try to understand the causes for escalating college costs. Underneath the trends of public opinion, however, lies another reason why existing colleges are maxed out. They are caught between the twin hammers of high personnel costs and depreciating facilities that require maintenance and replacement, and the anvil of higher tuition to balance the budgets. Committed to a campus-based economy, enhanced by a standing faculty and academic support staff, and confronted with declining institutional support from all government sources, colleges have only one card to play when they balance their budgets: higher tuition and fees.

In fact, the news that our education system is failing to serve these societal needs isn't news at all; it is a headlined, accepted truth. What has not been in the headlines is the fundamental cause of this failure. We have blamed the students, their parents, the society, the faculty, and other associated culprits who have been caught near the scene of the crime. In fact, however, colleges and universities in the twenty-first century don't work because they are maxed out. Organized around assumptions based in fourteenth-century Europe, they cannot amend their classic model sufficiently to reach beyond their current level of impact.

As Kevin Carey wrote in "What Colleges Should Learn from Newspapers' Decline," "Some people will argue that the best traditional college courses are superior to any online offering. ... But, remember, that's far from the experience of the lower-division undergraduate sitting in the back row of a lecture hall. All she's getting is a live version of what iTunes University offers for free, minus the ability to pause, rewind, and fast-forward at a time and place of her choosing ... She's also increasingly paying through the nose for the privilege" (2009, p. A21).

As the makeup of our learners diversifies, as American society becomes ever more digital and wired, as we are asked to become more successful with more learners, and as we prepare for the workforce needs required by our place in the global economy, the consequences of relying solely on outdated assumptions and models for all higher education becomes downright dangerous.

The consequences of the success ceiling won't be quiet much longer. Business leaders cry out in vain for higher education to equip employees to compete in a global marketplace. Legislators and community leaders watch school taxes and local college tuitions increase while graduation rates stagnate. And parents continue to watch children, colleagues, and relatives who are sunny and bright at home and work become quiet and unsuccessful at school.

What do we need to do to meet these challenges?

In the sixty years since the passage of the GI Bill—through the days of the civil rights movement, the rise of feminism, the advances in technology and space, the shrinking world, and the growing global economy—our strides toward achieving the American promise of opportunity in higher education have grown shorter. Although it is true that we are graduating more students than ever, our success rates are flattening as a percentage of the total population. We are winnowing out the very people we need if we, as a nation, want to compete in a global market. We are leaving behind millions of Americans who have the capacity to learn and for whom the promise of opportunity was made but not kept. We are wasting our talent.

As we look forward to the next twenty years and beyond, we must ask, *who* are we failing and *why*? Our relative failure lies in those parts of the population that are growing fastest. When asked to succeed with an ever-changing and expanding population of learners, diverse in their cultural experiences and educational preparation as well as their approaches to learning, our institutions gasp and struggle. The gasping is becoming more labored. We have increased undergraduate minority enrollments, but we have not fundamentally changed either the culture or the pedagogy—the means of learning—that could have accompanied this shift.

As a result, the struggle is not producing the results we need. Stated simply, *none* of our nation's student populations, especially minority students, are achieving college degrees at rates commensurate with their capacities and at levels acceptable to sustain society's long-term well-being. When one combines the population increases for minorities with the disparity between ethnicities in regard to college achievement, we are becoming a nation split by educational and occupational differences. Unless we can apply appropriate models of education for all of these students, we will not deliver on the promise that holds America together—a seat at the table of social, civic, and economic opportunity that rises from learning.

American higher education as we know it is "maxed out." The Law of Thirds, an indicator of stagnant success, represents the Law of Diminishing Returns at work in traditional higher education. The Law of Diminishing Returns holds that every model has its limitations, an outside limit to its performance. There are many constraints that come with this historic approach to educating people in college. In short, given these constraints, the current system is operating as successfully as it can.

The only way to break through the success ceiling is to be much more successful educating higher percentages of the existing population. But our colleges and universities have had only limited success doing this for the last thirty years. During this period of time, our results have stalled while the need has grown dramatically.

As Michael Porter (2008) wrote in *Businessweek*, "U.S. colleges and universities are precious assets, but we have no serious plan to improve access to them by our citizens. America now ranks twelfth among all nations in college education attainment for twenty-five to thirty-four-year-olds. We have made no progress in this vital area over the past thirty years, unlike almost every other country. This is an ominous trend in an economy that must have the skills to justify its high wages."

If the workforce were water in a tub, we have failed to fill the tub to the level needed. On top of that, unfortunately, the tub is currently leaking water out faster than we are putting water in. Workers are retiring at a rate faster than our skill and knowledge base is being renewed, creating a widening capacity gap relative to the growing demands of the domestic and global economies.

In the recent past, we have papered over the gap with H1B visas bringing foreign workers in while also moving jobs overseas, obscuring our failure to develop our own workforce. But our reliance on H1B visas will be less and less successful. First of all, they will be increasingly difficult to get in the current anti-immigration environment. Second, Indian and Chinese engineers, previously satisfied with life in the American diaspora, will be more likely to remain in or return to their native countries as opportunities expand there.

This book offers a new perspective on the cost of standing still as others gain on us. From this perspective, global "catch-up" to the United States in education attainment is a tsunami of threat headed directly at America's social, civic, and economic life. And we are standing on the beach, looking out to sea, with our feet in the sand, hoping that doing a better job with more of the same will save the day. We must understand that part of our education performance problem is a model that has reached its limits of effectiveness.

Yet, so far, as we lose ground to other countries in this education achievement sweepstakes, the explanations of why we are falling back echo a familiar litany of social and economic causes.

American higher education is the most comprehensive system in the world. Other countries are copying it as I write. But stalling success rates and rising costs have plagued postsecondary education for several years in the United States. Legislators have called for more accountability and better metrics to understand the value, efficiency, and effectiveness of higher education. And members of the academy, while working to satisfy demands for greater accountability, have suggested that more money, better spent on equipment; lower class sizes; and other initiatives will be necessary to solve the problem of stalled levels of results.

Both sides are right. But both sides are also missing a crucial point. The problem is not that colleges aren't working. Nor is it that learners aren't capable. The problem is that we are asking our dominant educational model to do more than any one approach can do successfully. Our colleges, as an educational model, have matured to the point of diminishing returns. Effectiveness and efficiency limitations have set in, and additional investment, no matter how necessary, will generate only marginal gains.

Our vision for higher education is too limited. If we are serious about dramatically increasing success rates in higher education, bringing millions of people from the margin of America's economy to its mainstream, America must adopt radically new understandings of effective teaching and learning in the twenty-first century, while keeping its current system in place and operating smoothly. We must build a new bicycle while riding the old one.

Why can't American colleges and universities just do more and do it better? If only it were that simple. Unfortunately, like Gulliver, they are tied down. But not with rope. In this case, the constraints are self-imposed: customs, conditions, and practices that have, even while evolving, hardened into place, like solder after the welder's flame has been extinguished. And then, with the practices fixed and unyielding, the environment has changed, demanding different services to meet the needs of new learners. Here are three factors that contribute to the Law of Diminishing Returns, ensuring that the mainstream of our current higher education system won't solve this problem.

There are not and will not be enough faculty members trained and available to teach the new learners. When I was serving as assistant director general for education at UNESCO, a study was completed concerning the future supply of faculty at all levels in sub-Saharan Africa. It concluded that, even if all the training programs currently in place operated at maximum efficiency and effectiveness, the African subcontinent faced a growing deficit of trained teachers compared to the need. It would have been easy to attribute this loss in trained teachers to rapidly expanding student population growth, deaths due to HIV/AIDS, and poor quality in the training programs. But the reasons behind the projected loss also included other, better paying possibilities for people with training. In Africa, a higher level of education gives the individual more power and mobility. Losing teachers to other parts of the economy is not just an African problem. We have the same problem right here in America.

The system is caught in the collision of two forces. Faculty, along with the traditions and incentives that they enjoy, experience limited pay and difficult working conditions. On the one hand, there is a limit to the number of people with master's and doctoral degrees who will settle for that life when the opportunities on the other side of the ivy wall are more attractive economically and, in many cases, more challenging intellectually. On the other hand, there is increasing demand for credentialed people outside of education. Well-trained people are more richly rewarded outside the education system than inside. For years Americans have debated the need to pay all teachers more. But there is no political will or calculus to achieve that goal.

One challenge for the twenty-first century is figuring out how to educate these new learners without an equivalent increase in faculty.

There won't be enough facilities. Campuses are expensive, not only to build but also to maintain. Like our interstate highway system, and the roads and bridges built before them during the depression by government-supported workers, there is a huge existing infrastructure that needs support. The liability of deferred maintenance coupled with the soaring cost of new facilities are an enormous weight on the budget of most American colleges today.

When an interstate bridge collapses, it makes news, at least for a week. The gasoline tax, at least, provides a continuing, if insufficient, source of money to fix the structure. But buildings are routinely added to college campuses without anyone providing the funds to cover depreciation and basic maintenance and upkeep. Without careful financial planning, there is no ready source of revenue to fix the leaky roof and pay the electrical bills.

The unfunded liability of college grounds and facilities is an enormous and growing burden on parents, students, alumni, and taxpayers alike. To make things worse, building maintenance just isn't very sexy. So, when faced with a choice between funding increased student assistance and fixing a laboratory, most legislators and donors will choose the student. Put bluntly, there is no political instinct to finance the facilities and support services needed to double the size or number of campuses.

Politics and constituencies' resistance will block change at existing institutions. Although we don't think of it this way, most institutions have a "brand" with their students, their faculty, their alumni, and their community. When MIT decided to put their undergraduate courses online for free in the OpenCourseWare project, there was some concern among faculty and others that it would weaken the institution's reputation. In general, however, it was considered a leadership act and generated wide and favorable publicity for MIT.

Then, however, some of the learners who had taken the courses offered began coming back to MIT looking for a way to have their informal learning assessed for academic credit. These requests were received coolly and with great caution by MIT. These self-learners' requests were denied. As the finest science and technology university in the world, MIT's brand would not permit them to certify that learning with academic credit.

Unless the survival of the institution is at stake, the alumni and core faculty will instinctively cling to the nostalgia and the values of the institution's history. And even if survival is at stake, sometimes they won't compromise.

Change that comes through government channels is equally hard to achieve. Political constituencies are always more finely tuned to what they are losing (unless they are on the outside looking in), than what they are gaining. And, typically, people who will benefit from significant change have far less political power than those opposing it. So, political change usually evolves incrementally, as an addition to the status quo, with compromises on both sides. Though it is a better way to proceed in some cases, this attitude would not have succeeded in the development of the personal computer or other disruptive breakthroughs in technology, and it will not succeed in winning the war on wasted talent.

The next chapter, "The Paradox of Personal Learning," paints a picture of the reality for millions of learners in America today, capturing the pain and the costs of unrecognized talent and accomplishment. The exquisite irony of the situation we face is that the institutions that got us where we are won't be able to finish the job—getting us where we need to go. We must build future solutions based on a different set of assumptions, realities, and knowledge. These ideas include the following:

- Talent is a natural, renewable resource.
- Personal learning is the way that talent is refreshed and renewed.
- We cannot afford to waste our talent any longer.
- The Law of Thirds must be reversed.
- Traditional institutions are maxed out.

If we are going to double the number of students in programs and also double successful completions, we need our existing colleges and universities to keep doing what they've been doing. They are the base on which we build, the maypole around which we dance. Their major focus should be to hold on to the educational progress we have made to date and focus on improving academic success rates with the new populations that are coming through their doors. Our traditional institutions need to "hold the line," to use Joshua Chamberlain's famous phrase at Gettysburg.

3

The Paradox of Personal Learning

Is there a pool of talent to draw from out there in America's communities and countryside? You bet there is.

Millions of American adults lead active, successful, and productive lives. They are talented. They work productively, read books, and attend courses and seminars. The learning that comes from these instinctive activities, which are embedded in the larger life experience, is one of the major ways that we renew and refresh our talent.

Yet, when it comes to getting a college degree, millions of these capable personal learners hit a dead end. Adults have been given many reasons why failure to go to or persist in college is their fault: lack of drive, family, economics, poor preparation, poor public schools, and low intelligence. None of these is a sufficient explanation for the casualty rate our learners experience. It is a cultural axiom that failure to persist in college is the fault of the learner, largely based on a flaw in the capacity, the life, or the background of each individual. In fact, however, lack of college success has as much or more to do with our colleges' historic practices, policies, and structures as it does with students' capacity to learn.

Allen Tough, a Canadian researcher, captured the way that we learn personally and how often we do it in *The Adult's Learning Projects* (1971): "Almost everyone undertakes at least one or two major learning projects a year. Some people undertake as many as fifteen or twenty. The median is eight projects a year lasting a total of eight hundred hours (fifteen hours a week)."

As an adult learner, you are the headline actor in your own personal drama, not a patient waiting for treatment. This learning and the human capacity that it reflects has strong human—as well as economic, civic, and social—value.

Learning, including college learning, is a force in every person's life. Too often, we write about adult lifelong learning and workforce education as if learning were an abstraction, something that happened to someone else. Devoid of the human realities that influence lifelong learning, we discuss colleges instead of people, policies instead of pain, formulas instead of the frustration that comes from being excluded. As a result, readers miss the yeasty stuff of daily life that lies beneath and informs all learning.

Far from being an abstraction, learning can be active, fun, redemptive, life changing, difficult, and very personal. Personal learning is the knowledge you gain from the totality of your life experiences, including school and formal training. It is the way you recover from adversity, ease transitions, and respond to opportunities. Personal learning develops actual skills and abilities that are marketable. It also helps you develop values, attitudes, and behaviors through reflection and introspection. This learning is an untapped natural resource of great importance to each of us, as well as to a society that says it values individual worth and promotes opportunity.

Imagine, then, the excruciating, negative impact on all those people who suffer from an "inability to thrive" in our schools and colleges.

It was when I was speaking to audiences about my earlier book, *The Quiet Crisis*, in 2004 that I first understood the human dimension lying behind the Law of Thirds. In my remarks, I would ask my audiences a question: "How many of you know someone—a son, daughter, brother, sister, neighbor, friend—who is bright, alert, lively, and, well ... who seems smart at home, at work, or in the neighborhood? And yet the same person becomes quiet, morose, reserved, hesitant, and, well ... dumb when he or she goes to school?" Without exception, most of the hands in the room would go up. Then I would ask, "And how many of you have felt that way yourselves?" More than half of the hands would go up again.

Wherever I presented *The Quiet Crisis*, whether in rotary clubs, higher education audiences, policy groups, or more public gatherings, the response was the same. Everyone knew someone who was "smart at home, but dumb in school." Few people remembered education as enjoyable. And most, whether they had been successful or not, remembered it as a set of experiences that was defined as much by frustration as it was by hope, and by who failed as much as by who succeeded.

This is the human side of the Law of Thirds in American education. It is defined not by peoples' capacity to learn but as a consequence of the way colleges are structured. Like an invisible hand, it limits the opportunity for adult learners to attain an associate's degree or more. Millions of adult learners who are smart and capable in their daily professional, civic, and social lives become frustrated and "dumb" when it comes to persisting and succeeding in college.

It doesn't have to be this way. American learners are much more capable than the "success ceiling" allows. There are solutions that will allow America to educate millions of people to higher levels. Chris Anderson's theory of the "Long Tail" applies to curricular content and organized learning opportunities in higher education. Anderson writes, "The theory of the Long Tail is that our culture and economy is increasingly shifting away from a focus on a relatively small number of 'hits' (mainstream products and markets) at the head of the demand curve and toward a huge number of niches in the tail. As the costs of production and distribution fall, especially online, there is now less need to lump products and consumers into one-size-fits-all containers. In an era

without the constraints of physical shelf space and other bottle-
necks of distribution, narrowly targeted goods and services can be
as economically attractive as mainstream fare" (Anderson, 2006).

Higher education's emerging Long Tail—diverse, accessible,
and virtually unlimited content—coupled with powerful technologies are making personalized and adaptive learning available on a
scale that has heretofore been unimaginable. It upends our conventional understanding of content and the presentation of curriculum. What you learn, when and where you learn it, and how
you learn it are negotiable variables in the new education paradigm. Adapting to the needs, styles, and situations of the learners
will become the norm, not the exception.

When we blend the Long Tail theory with American folklore,
things begin to get interesting. Our folklore is filled with the
mythology of learning and opportunity. Born of phrases and stories,
this mythology is the keystone to the American Dream, delivering
its message again and again.

Live and Learn

The School of Hard Knocks

The Horatio Alger Story

Rags to Riches

In each case, the message is similar. You can learn from the
experience of living. There are strong and useful connections
between effort, learning, and success. If you are resourceful, work
hard, and learn on your feet, opportunity will come knocking.
Learning that is personal and customized to your needs is more
accessible than ever before.

Part of the mythology is correct. Most of us do learn actively
and purposefully on an ongoing basis. And, to avoid any confusion
in your mind, colleges account for only part of that learning. You
are learning when you do any of the following:

- You read about child development and discuss parenting with a friend or an organized group in order to cope better with the children in your life.

- You take a series of courses at work to be certified in a new application process.

- Your supervisor at work demonstrates a new technique or the company brings in a lecturer to describe a new development in the industry.

- You develop a health and diet plan to keep physically fit while eating well.

- You read several books on China or Mexico to know more about those countries or to plan a trip.

- You take several courses through continuing education.

- You buy a new computer with expanded capacity and spend time learning how to use the new software and the capacity it contains.

- You learn to play an instrument, engage in therapy, or learn a new sport.

This learning has three important characteristics.

It is always personal. Learning is shaped to and by our uniqueness. One person is moved to tears upon hearing the story of Lincoln's childhood, whereas another yawns. A young woman, recently orphaned, reads a psychology text in ways that a retired autoworker, who has returned to college for a few classes, cannot imagine—and the inverse is equally true. One person's revelation about culture and diversity is another's confirmation. We learn as we are, influenced by our fears and our faiths and our singular experiences.

It is always purposeful. Learning happens because we want it to. We read and remember the essence of a passage because it explains our lives a little bit, we think it's perceptive, and we want to quote it to someone else. We admire a skill or resource someone else has, and want to learn it ourselves. We may forget why we first started; we may shift what we value most; but if we are, in fact, learning, it is because each of us, as an individual, wants and needs to learn.

It is always powerful. Learning, unlike nearly anything else, bears down on us in ways that change us: it revises how we think, how we feel, how we behave. It yields new skills with which we can surprise or delight others and ourselves. It enables us to rise above our places in society by showing others our unique, hidden credentials. Even if we are not thinking about what we are doing as learning—checking an old recipe in a worn cookbook, reading a journal, seeing a counselor—it is, in fact, what we are doing.

Consider the case of Connie, a personal learner who was able to respond to her boss's request.

> Connie felt pretty darn good. She knew she could do pretty much anything she put her mind to. So, Mr. Driscoll, her boss, wanted her to go into sales and learn the marketing side of the business. She had done things like that before, learning from the bottom up. There was the time when her boss at the bank needed someone to help out checking loans. So, he asked her to do it. Connie began looking at the loans immediately, to get a feel for what they were like. Then she added a short course at the Institute, a couple of books and articles, and continuing conversations with her colleagues. The experience, coupled with the outside learning, soon gained her a reputation as one of the best.

But the other part of the myth—that personal learning paves the pathway to opportunity—has become a casualty of higher education practice and policy in our country. Despite the abundance of knowledge described by the Long Tail theory, the abundance of learning identified by Allen Tough, and the folklore that says we believe in the value of personal learning, most colleges simply ignore experience and personal learning as they prepare students for a set of life opportunities that require credits, certificates, and degrees. The worker's training on the job, the mother's experience with her children, the soldier's training as a commander, the Peace Corps volunteer's training in water engineering and exposure to a foreign culture are largely ignored as important learning and as an educational base on which to build. Sometimes, if you get lucky, you can successfully transfer credit earned at one school to another, and get it all counted toward your degree requirements, earning advanced placement for subjects you have already studied at another institution. But transferring learning done outside of college into college is a far more difficult, far chancier affair.

Peg's life story gives a good example of personal learning. Two of her children were asthmatic and she wanted better health care service for them. So, she attended a meeting on community health care issues. Soon after, with only a high school diploma and a commitment to the area where her roots ran deep, Boston's Old North End, Peg became the director of a new health care center there. Listen as she describes her personal learning and the awkward distance that she feels from formal education.

> I think I changed around the time I took this job. I used to be very much in awe of people. If someone were a doctor or a lawyer or a teacher, it was like, "Oh my god, they're better than I am." Working in this job, I found that everyone is a human being. I had to stop being in awe of people and begin to feel as if I were on the same level so that I could be successful at what I was trying to do. As a result, my negotiating skills with these people became much stronger.

I learn from other people. I am not a particularly good reader. When I go to meetings, it's at the breaks and after the meeting that I get a wealth of information, because I talk to you and you tell me what you're doing. I've picked up an incredible amount from people that way.

I was able to accomplish a lot without the paper [a baccalaureate degree], more power to me. But I think the important component of the whole thing is that if you have an education with no common sense (and there is nothing I know of in any school that teaches you that) then you really do have a worthless piece of paper. I know I've learned something when I can take it and apply it to something else. Then, I've learned it.

Now listen to Bob, a different story with very similar themes. Bob is a short, peppery man with more of a "rags to riches" story to tell. He was stifled in his early adult years, a victim of his circumstances, powerless and controlled by the events of his life. But when he came home after a tour of duty in the army, the travel, his reading, and his personal experiences had given him a ray of hope that "somewhere along the line, something would work out."

Successful at work as a fireman, Bob had done an enormous amount of learning. But, initially, he lacked the confidence that he could possibly be a learned person. Then, later, he concluded that his personal learning would never be enough. Without a formal education, his career path would be blocked.

When you're programmed to be a loser for seventeen years, you don't stop being a loser just because someone says you're not a loser. It doesn't work that way. You think about it and you say, "Hey, maybe he's right. I hope he's right," but you just don't know what to do.

Among other things, about fifteen years ago I started to read. I had never read a book, an entire book. But then I began to read. I read anything, mostly what people might say is nonfiction because there was so much stuff that I didn't know. And then people began plugging me into other stuff.

What happens is that, at some point, someone identifies that you've got untapped skills, and no one knows another way to develop them than school. You've never heard anybody grab anybody and talk to him like a Dutch Uncle. Put their arm around him and say, "Listen kid, you've got what it takes, you ought to go to the library and read a book"—people just don't say it!

What they do say is that college will get you ahead. Like my boss told me, "You need this. It's the only way out. You're going to be wasted if you don't get this." I don't care how bright you are, you don't get into the club unless you wear the ring. Out of all the all-stars, 99 percent will wear the ring.

There are millions of people just like Peg, Bob, and Connie. They personalize two truths: people learn all the time and have significant capacities, yet, in far too many cases, these capacities are invisible to the outside world, including to colleges and universities. Their stories radiate the positive and powerful force of personal learning as the natural resource that people harness to continually rewrite their life scripts. And they make the case that understanding what you have learned is powerful personally and should be recognized educationally.

Personal learning is the way we breathe in new ideas, new behaviors, and new knowledge and exhale the old. It acts as our internal gyroscope, creating balance out of imbalance, while allowing us to adapt to and cope with new situations, demands, and opportunities. Such learning may be pleasant or unpleasant, difficult or easy, but it is not incidental. It is not the frosting, it's the cake.

Whether or not most people are aware of the personal learning they have done, at some point we all recognize that we have changed over the years. This recognition can range from a casual observation of the characteristics of aging to a more profound understanding of growth and development.

Personal learning is our natural way of developing our talent. If that talent goes untapped, however, if that renewable resource is ignored, America's talent pool is diminished, with enormous costs and consequences for our society.

This anonymous blog response I received in early 2009 says it all.

> I have taken some college courses, but found more benefit from the education I received on the job, or from life experience. Many people I know have obtained a college degree simply because it is the first requirement listed in a job posting. ... The other part of the problem is that most bachelor's degree programs require four years of commitment. ... I have never understood why obtaining a degree must require four years. We waste a lot of effort, time, and money. Institutions should feel free to incorporate general education skills into their major-specific courses.
>
> Now, once you have the education, there is another issue. Many companies require a certain amount of experience in the field before they will hire you, because our degree programs do not educate students on everything they need to know in the real world. So, you've lost out on four years of experience in the field while attending school and now you have to find a company that will employ you without the experience, usually low-paying positions or internships. So—in the end—it could well take six to eight years before students can afford to pay back their student loans.
>
> So, why am I here? Well, I suppose I've hit a wall. I cannot go much further in my field without a degree.

Not for a lack of knowledge, skill, or ambition, but because I don't have a piece of paper saying I wasted those four years in school. I now must find the fastest way to a degree because most companies in my field require that you have a bachelor's degree for the positions I am eligible for. I have actually had companies tell me that I "would be perfect for the position, but HR requires that you have a degree." Not "a degree or equivalent experience" … a piece of paper. Like a passport to a career that comes with a hefty price.

In college, all learners are treated essentially the same way, sitting in lectures, reading and taking notes, doing homework. But when we learn personally, we adapt to our natural "strong suits" for learning. We learn in whatever ways we learn best. Howard Gardner's research on multiple intelligences tells us that we each have distinct ways of interpreting the world. Instead of forcing us into the straitjacket of someone else's way of doing it, personal learning allows us to move freely on our own (1983). By knowing how we learn, by learning the importance of reflection, we can make conscious learning a lifelong process while connecting it with an appropriate degree or certificate.

This suggests another way of thinking about organizing for learning in the twenty-first century. As we think about the different possibilities, however, it is important to look beyond our existing institutions. If we asked the existing higher education model to solve this problem, we would be indulging ourselves and basing our policy on a conceit. A conceit is defined as "excessive appreciation of one's own worth or virtue."

In Part Two, "Dangerous Conceits," we will discuss three additional reasons why the traditional higher educational model, as good as it is, is simply not positioned to meet this new challenge and win the war on wasted talent. To think otherwise would be a dangerous conceit.

Part II

Dangerous Conceits

The dynamic, evolving story of American history is filled with examples of customs, societal habits, or practices that, having been embedded in social practice in one era, were rejected in the next. As a general characteristic, we have experienced successive intergenerational transfers of power and access since the first days of the new republic. Through this process, privileges and opportunities that were scarce to the poor and less powerful in one generation became more available in future generations.

This ever-widening circle of access and inclusion to previously withheld social and economic benefits has repeatedly proved, renewed, and strengthened the American promise of opportunity. This is as true for paid vacations and ownership of a car and a home as it is for equal rights before the law and education.

Higher education has been no exception to this intergenerational transfer of power. The role of the university itself has evolved from the era of educating ministers and philosophers at only a very few elite private schools to the land grant revolution of the late nineteenth century. In the twentieth century, the GI Bill, community college movement, and Pell grant and Stafford loan revolutions once again transformed access, redefining who was welcome and encouraged to attend the colleges and universities of America.

At each step, forces of the status quo, like a finely tuned Greek chorus, warned of the impending calamity that would result from the arrival of new students, previously unserved.

- Community colleges would dilute the quality of the college graduate.
- The GI Bill would bring unqualified veterans into our colleges and universities.
- Funding students directly would undermine our institutions' stability.

Generally, the deeper, often-unspoken worry was that new policies would contribute to the end of western civilization as we knew it. And, in an ironic twist, they did, but in a hugely positive way. With each successive wave of new policies, programs, institutional forms, and students, America's talent pool deepened as new lives were touched and changed by education. The corollary benefits were that the country's promise of opportunity was reaffirmed while the strength of the society and its representative democracy were deepened and redefined. The time has come to do it again.

"Dangerous Conceits" analyzes some die-hard generational practices in higher education that block the pathway to opportunity for today's adult learners. They have persisted, even as the world around our colleges and universities has changed dramatically. And they need to change. These conceits make getting a higher education, and the acknowledgment that comes with it, far more difficult for millions of learners. Although they are accepted customs of the academy, in practice they hold capable learners away from the social, civic, and economic rewards that are conferred by success in higher education. In blunter terms, they waste talent.

People with wasted talent are personal learners who have been ignored. They are your friends and neighbors, cousins and colleagues. And they are waiting for the talent-friendly college of the twenty-first century, at which learning environments support the way they learn best; assessment services diagnose how they learn best and validate the learning they have completed outside of college; and the formal learning they have already accomplished is recognized and valued, not penalized and discounted.

Many of these underserved learners share one or both of two characteristics that define their lives and limit America's future. They have *untapped potential*, capacity that neither they nor higher education institutions recognize. The undiscovered artist. The future teacher who never could go to college. The real estate salesman who might be a software engineer. Insurance saleswomen who might be scientists. They might have *untapped knowledge* as well. Draftsmen who know enough to become architects. Aides with extensive experience who might become teachers or nurses.

"Untapped potential" is a gentle way of referring to people with the capacity to learn who are shut out by the way we teach and by the organization and time structures of our colleges. In Chapter Four, "Different Strokes for Different Folks," we see the costs and the consequences of continuing to insist that all learning occur within the traditional collegiate teaching-learning environment.

"Untapped knowledge" refers to capacities that are already developed but that remain unrecognized and unacknowledged because the credentials given by higher education have been withheld. This lack of recognition limits the learner's access to higher levels at work and education. In Chapter Five, "Learning Is More Than Strictly Academic," we will discuss the personal and societal costs of continuing to leave people's knowledge untapped. These learners need to have their knowledge assessed and recognized and to gain advanced placement in college for what they already know.

Finally, Chapter Six, "You Can't Get There from Here," discusses the ultimate conceit: withholding recognition of learning recognized and accomplished in other accredited institutions. Even if you tap your potential and your knowledge, this dangerous conceit discounts your learning every time you move from one institution to another. And, in an increasingly mobile society, attending more than one institution has become the norm, not the exception.

As the Gates Foundation reported in a 2008 study, more than half the money spent on higher education in the United States, including the more than $100 billion a year for financial aid, does not lead to any degree or credential (Wallis, 2008). This is, in part, the hidden financial cost of these "dangerous conceits": practices and learning environments that are not friendly to the students who attend college.

The dangerous conceits discussed in this section are examples of current practices that keep many capable people away from higher education while making it extremely difficult for those who actually get there to succeed and finish. They are three reasons among many that explain why so many Americans hit the success ceiling, becoming casualties of the Law of Thirds.

4

Different Strokes for Different Folks

A man named Joe wrote the following response to my blog: "I'm one of those people who slipped through the cracks of education. For years, I thought I was probably just 'dumb.' Then, around my early forties, I realized that I loved to learn. It was the traditional school setting that didn't work for me. Over the last fifteen years, I have traveled the world—thirty-five trips to twenty-seven countries. This has given me tremendous insights and the opportunity to learn a myriad of things."

Some people might try to argue that Joe just slipped through the cracks. Joe didn't "slip through the cracks"; he was, in all likelihood, shuffled out of the deck. For years, colleges and universities have been able to duck basic questions: Why do so many apparently capable people fail to thrive in their classrooms and on their campuses, their potential untapped? How is it that people who go on to lead productive and thoughtful lives of accomplishment were unable to find the right groove in college and push through to successful completion as a younger person? Or, even when they are armed with additional experience, learning, and the increased ability to focus that can develop over time, why do so many older adult learners simply drift with the tides of life, choosing not to engage with the college of their choice?

For one reason, colleges have historically seen the rejection and failure of students as a necessary part of their business. A key part of the collegiate identity has been based on who was denied entry and who did not succeed within their walls. Colleges have been able to justify their rates of failure because part of their accepted societal role has been to winnow out "less capable" students, leaving the value of higher education available to those who, so the belief went, could "benefit" from it.

Although social and economic status have continued to play a role in assigning who will "benefit" from higher education, this selectivity has also been justified in part by the concept of meritocracy. Thomas Jefferson imagined, indeed the mythic American Dream was based on, an understanding of the world as a place where people would rise to the top based on their capacities and their merits, not their stations in life. Since that time, meritocracy has been used as an underlying logic for winnowing out less qualified people in a competition with other people for a limited number of opportunities. It has been perceived as a doctrine of fairness, based on merit and applied human capacity.

Regardless of the intention lying behind this approach, the application of meritocracy in education has entailed a huge cost. Millions of people, who were otherwise qualified, were either denied access to or were simply left out of college, losing the value of the experience and the knowledge that came with it. Their human potential remained officially untapped. Like Bob in the previous chapter, they felt like economic and social castaways before they ever had a chance to compete. This practice was tolerated as de facto public policy until the GI Bill was passed, bringing tens of thousands of returning veterans into our colleges and universities.

But there was a second reason why the impact of meritocracy in education was as accepted as the air we breathe: there were limited opportunities in the workplace and limited spaces in colleges. So, on the one hand, education was not seen as a valuable thing, in and of itself. On the other hand, exclusion from education was justified by the scarcity of careers for educated people.

Today, however, the situation has reversed itself. We know that people can and do learn all the time. And, as we saw in "Wasted Talent," America is generating more high-skilled job opportunities than there are qualified people to fill them. For the first time in American history, our need for educated members of the workforce is far greater than the available supply. We no longer need to winnow people out based on merit. We need to find, develop, and confirm the merit in people.

So, the educational challenge has been reversed. The days of winnowing are behind us. In this emerging environment, we are aiming at success with the middle third: those who have a high school diploma and no college experience. In approaching this population, we know that we need to maximize everyone's learning to the limits of their capacities. Merit is a goal, something to be enhanced and developed, a criterion of institutional success, not a criterion for exclusion. Achieving educational approaches that develop and recognize merit, validating capacity and knowledge, will require radically different educational commitments and practices.

But this new mind-set will be extremely difficult, if not impossible, for our colleges and universities to grasp, let alone embrace. Many faculty members know and attempt to integrate knowledge about how people learn into their curricula and teaching. The collective impact, however, is weakened by the inertia of institutions that simply cannot move fast enough for learners who are left out by the traditional frameworks.

When it comes to serving the middle third of students, colleges are caught in outdated practices—dangerous conceits—that make them far less capable of succeeding with the learners who historically have not had access to or been able to succeed in the traditional college model. The result is millions of people whose potential is untapped by a society that needs them. People with untapped potential either never show up or disappear from our schools before they graduate. They have the capacities to learn and to contribute, but they do not persist either in school or, many times, at work because the traditional learning environments in colleges are unfriendly to their styles, their intelligences, or their life patterns.

Knowing what we know about diseases of the blood, we would never suggest that a diabetic could successfully run a marathon without insulin. Medical science tells us that it would be a disaster. Yet, when we know that a person's learning style or "intelligence" profile is at odds with the way schools are run, we have done little or nothing. As a result, our colleges and universities have implicitly favored those people who learn well in the environments they offer. Seen from the other perspective, the dominant way that teaching and learning are hosted in the vast majority of our colleges and universities is not well matched with the learning styles and intelligence profiles of many potential students.

In this scenario, a "bad fit" between the learner and the college has been, effectively, the learner's responsibility. Although we might try to remediate learners' performance deficits, we have accepted little or no responsibility for understanding and acting on how they might learn better. With the information we now have about how people learn, however, this approach could be characterized as a case of bad professional practice. No matter what, it is bad news for the learner, the college, and the country.

And, as we learned from the Gates Foundation report on the expense incurred for noncompleters every year, it turns out to be expensive bad business as well (Wallis, 2008). In many cases, ironically, colleges have sponsored the very science that has made successful education possible for many more learners. But these same colleges are incapable of integrating that science into their practices. As a result, educational practices that reach back to the 1950s and earlier trump the knowledge of the twenty-first century.

I was raised in the American era of the 1950s. The structure and purposes of higher education were almost universally admired and accepted. In any dispute between professor and student, the professor was always on the side of the angels. And the larger rules in college were simple: they teach, you learn. Your formal education was the pathway to success. College was the platform from which one could dive into a successful life of work, service, and contribution. "Get your education and everything else will follow." That was the message.

Since the end of World War II, however, we have witnessed a staggering expansion of our knowledge about learning. Most of the evidence that we've accumulated about the way people learn contradicts the dominance of traditional and common practice in teaching and learning. It only partially supports the dominant academic model of colleges and universities. We know that although each person might approach learning differently, all people learn from their lived experiences—including the experience of school—whether they are positive or negative.

Yet, sadly, higher education has treated new and valued knowledge about why people learn and how they learn best like the modern doctor who, seeing a badly infected toe, calls for a bullet to bite and a saw. Most colleges and universities operate like an emergency room in which the first thing they do is put a splint on your arm, regardless of your complaint. Imagine the conversation.

"What happened to you?"

"My head and neck are killing me. I was whiplashed when my car was rear-ended."

"Okay. Let's just get this splint on your arm and then we'll talk."

Absurd? Absolutely. But when you are looking for an explanation of why more than two-thirds of our ninth graders have vanished from the education system by the age of twenty-three, without success in college, this is a good place to start. If there are multiple ways that people learn, and colleges emphasize labs and lectures, learners with capacities that fall outside the college model will be compromised, if not shut out entirely.

The Law of Thirds and the diminishing returns portrayed in stagnant success rates are driven by, among other things, a mismatch between the way people learn and the way colleges are organized.

Here are just three examples of relatively new knowledge about learning. They are part of a larger body of research that gives us the knowledge and the tools to put learners and their learning at the center of our teaching-learning focus. The research of Allen Tough, Howard Gardner, and Mary Meeker contribute different insights into a growing body of knowledge and thought that describe a new ecology of learning. In this new ecology, personal learning will be recognized as a natural, renewable resource, and the way you actually learn will be a critical element in the design and implementation of learning events. Both will be harnessed to drive more effective and successful learning for more people.

As I described earlier, Allen Tough defined a learning project as a concerted effort to learn new behaviors, skills, or knowledge. The average learning project consumes fifteen hours per week (1971). As he studied the phenomenon of learning projects, he discovered that people everywhere, across continents, cultures, and lifestyles, regardless of income and education level, were involved continuously in these learning projects. The average person conducted eight to ten such projects, consuming an average of more than seven hundred hours of learning each year.

Over time, Tough was able to fill out the picture of this recurring and natural, yet purposeful and focused, learning that we do. He identified that, without assistance, the learner sets a goal and then decides what he or she needs to learn, how best to achieve that learning, and when enough learning has occurred. Sometimes with the aid of a mentor, sometimes in a course or a workshop, sometimes at work, and sometimes proceeding alone, learners then would go to the library, seek out an expert, or ask for help from peers. Today, a learner would be equally likely to search the Web as the most available portal of information and knowledge. We all begin, pursue, and conclude learning projects, including those within more formal education systems.

Each project, and sometimes multiple projects, reflects a learning cycle, but you can think of it as a journey. In the first stage, you take stock of where you are and set a goal. Then you map out a plan, a way to get where you want to go. Then you make the trip. And, when you determine you have arrived, you have completed the exercise.

Three of my learning projects come to mind as examples. The first is the Community College of Vermont (CCV). When I started that institution with a small group of people, we designed and implemented the college with one thing in mind: putting student learning at the center. We were using community resources for our campuses and our faculty. Our curriculum was outcomes based. Everything we did was experimental, testing, adopting, evaluating, and rejecting as we went along. As I came to understand the concept of learning projects, I called CCV the "mother" of all learning projects.

Second, in my early days as the founding president of CCV, I realized that I simply did not possess the management experience to organize and lead the ever-expanding organization. After looking at several books and professional training seminars, I took another route. I asked an elder statesman of Vermont education, John Holden, to attend the college's management meetings and shadow me on a regular basis as a mentor and a guide. Holden knew the state, as a former superintendent and commissioner of education. He was respected as a professional and a manager. For over a year, he watched and mentored me as an educational leader, helping me understand some of the basics as well as the nuances of managing and leading. After about fourteen months, I had reached the level of comfort I was looking for, and John's service was concluded.

And third, a couple of years later, my lack of experience and formal knowledge about what a college president did was emerging again as a problem. Here I was, twenty-nine years old, with my master's degree in teaching, in the fifth year of running a new, but increasingly complex, institution. We were having tremendous success, but I was increasingly unsure of how to do my job well. This time, I thought, I needed more than a temporary advisor.

Through the good offices of a mutual friend and colleague, Blenda Wilson, I scheduled a conversation with the dean of the Harvard Graduate School of Education, Paul Ylvisaker. I told the dean that I needed help, but that his programs were not helpful to me because I was still doing my job. Furthermore, I continued, the job was a tremendous learning laboratory for management and leadership. I needed a way to combine my work and a doctoral program in a seamless way.

Ylvisaker's answer solved my problem and changed the course of my professional life. He said, "Well, Peter, we have a little-used option here at the Harvard Graduate School of Education, 'Special Student' status. We will assign you an advisor, Frederic Jacobs. Together, you and he will design a course of study that meets your needs. There will be no requirements in the course distribution or content. But you will have to complete the requisite number of courses, and fulfill all the writing requirements, including the thesis, to meet the degree requirements."

In other words, I was going to be allowed to use my work setting as a laboratory for my learning. I could select courses and create independent studies that answered the questions and responded to the problems arising at work.

At its heart, my doctoral work in administration, planning, and social policy revolved around the question of why CCV was suc-ceeding. I studied organizational culture, strategic planning, lead-ership, management, assessment, and related subjects as I expanded my understanding based on the actual life experience I was having. My study and learning became an integrated part of my life, not a separate activity.

The conceit of our colleges' and universities' dominant model is that they dictate the pattern of the actual activity of learning, divorcing it from the instincts and experience of the learner. In this practice, learners are asked to drop what they are doing and to ignore their own deep questions about learning and life, as well as what they already know, as the price of participation. Although this logic might work for some eighteen-year-olds, I believe that ignoring the best, natural way that each person learns doesn't hold water as an approach. For older students, it makes even less sense. Colleges need to understand that how the activity of learning is staged and supported is, in and of itself, a powerful educational tool.

How your intelligence works, however, is quite distinct from the activity of learning, so beautifully defined by Allen Tough. We now understand that intelligence, the stuff that characterizes the capacity to learn, has several faces. Howard Gardner authored *Frames of Mind* in 1983. In it, he began to develop his theory of multiple intelligences, identifying and describing several different ways that we, as individuals, use intelligence to experience and understand the world around us. For example, you may be strong in areas of logic and verbal skills, whereas others are more kinesthetic, visual, or interpersonal learners. But each form of intelligence is a distinct way of experiencing the world (in other words, of learning). There's no better or worse; no right or wrong.

Clayton Christiansen described and analyzed Gardner's definition of intelligence in his provocative and illuminating book, *Disrupting Class* (2008). According to Christiansen, intelligence is:

- the ability to solve problems that one encounters in real life,

- the ability to generate new problems to solve, and

- the ability to make something or offer a service that is valued in one's culture.

This definition escapes the narrow clutches of an IQ score. In studying intellectual capacity, Gardner established criteria to aid him in deciding whether a talent that could be observed was actually a distinct intelligence, and therefore whether it merited its own spot in his categorization scheme. His criteria are that "each intelligence must have a developmental feature, be observable in such special populations as prodigies or 'savants,' provide some evidence of localization in the brain, and support a symbolic or notational system." From this, Gardner originally came up with seven distinct intelligences. He has since added an eighth to that list and given consideration to a couple more.

Gardner's (1983) eight intelligences, with brief definitions, are:

- *Linguistic:* Ability to think in words and use language to express complex meanings.

- *Logistical-Mathematical:* Ability to calculate, quantify, consider propositions and hypotheses, and perform complex mathematical operations.

- *Spatial:* Ability to think in three-dimensional ways, perceive external and internal imagery, recreate, and transform. Or modify images, navigate oneself and objects through space, and produce or decode graphic information.

- *Bodily-kinesthetic:* Ability to manipulate objects and fine-tune physical skills.

- *Musical:* Ability to distinguish and create pitch, melody, rhythm, and tone.

- *Interpersonal:* Ability to understand and interact effectively with others.

- *Intrapersonal:* Ability to construct an accurate self-perception and to use this knowledge in planning and directing one's life.

- *Naturalist:* Ability to observe patterns in nature, identify and classify objects, and understand natural and human-made systems.

How does this relate to teaching and learning? When an educational approach is well aligned with one's stronger intelligences or aptitudes, understanding can come more easily and with greater enthusiasm. To put it differently, the learning can be intrinsically motivating (Christiansen, 2008, p. 25).

Howard Gardner argues that the big challenge facing the deployment of human resources is "how to best take advantage of the uniqueness conferred on us as a species exhibiting several intelligences" (Gardner, 1983).

So, an intrapersonal learner might well work better alone or in small groups, whereas a visual learner might be more likely to have to "see it to get it." The artist and the mathematician see and experience the world differently. The introvert and the extrovert work differently. The naturalist and the athlete react instinctively in different ways to phenomena around them. We know that each of us has a personal learning portrait that is as distinct from others' as a Monet from a Picasso, or a comic cartoon from an architect's design.

Gardner has emphasized this point: instead of emphasizing how *intelligent* we are, our focus should be on *how* we are intelligent.

If I am ever tempted to ignore the reality of multiple intelligences, I think of a class I taught while I was president of California State University, Monterey Bay. We had created an entry seminar for freshmen called the ProSeminar, which was intended to assist incoming students in their educational and professional planning. One of the key elements was helping each student grasp a fundamental understanding of how he or she learned. I taught Gardner's multiple intelligences to encourage students to consider how each of them learned differently. We used small-group discussions and simple exercises to elicit the perceived alignment of the different intelligences for each learner.

Branded in my mind is the image of a young Latino student's hand waving in class immediately after he'd initially digested the meaning, for him, of one aspect of Gardner's multiple intelligence theory. Eyes flashing, voice quivering, he blurted out, "Is this why I had such a terrible time in high school math?" He understood, for the first time, that he had strong and weak ways of learning and that the structure of his high school's curriculum had worked against his natural strengths.

This young man had struggled in high school math because he experienced the world in ways other than the way the math was taught. It's not that he wasn't smart. Most of us know intuitively that we all learn differently from one another—through different methods, with different styles, and at different paces. As Gardner suggested, it is how we are intelligent that matters.

And now, just for a minute, imagine that we knew how to do three things.

- Inform the learner, his or her teacher, and the curriculum of the learner's cognitive strengths and weaknesses within his or her intelligence profile.

- Connect those strengths and weaknesses to specific parts of the learner's audio and visual processes.

- Once identified, strengthen the weaknesses, improving performance on specific intellectual activities.

Although it is only one of many assessment processes, Structure of Intellect (SOI) assessments can do these things, informing all parts of the teaching-learning equation. So, where did SOI come from?

During the early years of World War II, the U.S. army was having a difficult time retaining similarly qualified candidates in pilot training school. Within the population of healthy young men, whose weight, height, educational attainment, and IQ fell within prescribed ranges that portended success, there were significant performance differences in preflight training, with a resulting high drop-out rate.

Their interest aroused by what they saw as an unexplained anomaly, army officials started looking for other explanations for the wide variety of results from an apparently uniform candidate pool. Over the years, this research evolved into a body of thought and research called Structure of Intellect, based on the work of many, most notably J. P. Guilford (1956). In "The Structure of Intellect," he illustrated the deeper aspects of intellectual functioning and described a more comprehensive understanding of intellect and how it works than that represented by IQ tests.

Building off Guilford's ground-breaking research, Mary Meeker moved the spotlight from a focus on the assessment of learners' differing abilities to a focus on the development of those abilities so that learners functioned better. She wrote, "It would seem that teaching the ability to learn should be considered as equally important a goal as a mastery of prescribed content" (1969, p. 4).

In its current state, SOI can be employed to do the following things.

- It lays the foundation for the acquisition of specific academic skills. It helps a learner prepare to acquire curricular content.

- If a student lacks certain SOI abilities and, therefore, has difficulty learning, SOI training can provide the missing foundations for acquiring academic skills.

- A full understanding of SOI by the learner can provide pathways to new thinking and reasoning abilities. (Structure of Intellect Systems, 1982)

In this diagnostic process alone, we have the ability to do the following.

- Identify strengths and weaknesses associated with the use of specific intellectual skills.

- Strengthen the weaknesses and, in so doing, increase the learner's ability to employ those intellectual skills.

- Tie that profile of learning to specific curricula and pedagogical approaches, maximizing the chances for success.

- Link the learner to careers that will align well with
  his or her intellectual structure.

The significance of this level of knowledge has an impact on how we would structure a learning environment across the board. As only one example, it redefines the meaning and the potential for remediation. Remediation today focuses on improving a student's academic activity—writing, reading, computation—not on strengthening the underlying weak intellectual skill. So, to give a very simple example, if a person had a weakness in his or her eye muscles, and the resulting inability to track their eyes from left to right to read a line of print affected his or her ability to read at a high, or even functional, level, practice that strengthened the eye muscles would deepen that individual's ability to read.

Looking at learning through the lens of Allen Tough's, Howard Gardner's, and Mary Meeker's research, we are reminded that, since 1950, we have learned more about and understand better how people learn than we did in all the preceding years. And we know that although each person might approach learning differently, all people learn from their lived experiences.

Understanding the different mosaics of intelligence within people, the different combinations and nuances of how individuals approach understanding and experience the world around them, opens the door to wide varieties of educational responses. It allows us, as educators, to be more like orchestra conductors than managers of information distribution.

We know that a doctor would not dream of prescribing medication or recommending treatment without taking the time to learn important diagnostic information about the patient. In higher education, however, where we now have the capacity to do the same kind of diagnosis with every learner, we typically look the other way and do this year what we did last year.

When learners engage in much of their personal learning, they will adapt instinctively to ways of learning that work to their benefit, learning naturally according to their styles and strengths. So, when Peg worked at the community mental health center, she learned naturally, according to her style and strengths. That's not, however, the way most colleges think about learning when they create a curriculum or train a faculty member. When you go to college, you trade flexibility for organized content, a standard teaching style, and academic recognition. In most cases, colleges build their curricula in an intellectual hierarchy that bears no resemblance to how learning actually happens in daily life. Furthermore, they offer that material in a format that asks dynamic and active learners to do it their way or no way at all.

When I presented the Law of Thirds earlier, I used statistics to describe the failure of our education system to respond to individual learning needs. We can now imagine the impact of the Law of Thirds in human terms, understanding the waste that results from our trying to drive square pegs into round holes in American higher education. When we recognize the human dimension of the roughly 70 percent of all ninth graders who are spun out of the system, we are looking at the splinters and chips from those millions of square pegs.

Allen Tough described *how* people go about learning, the learning project. Howard Gardner outlined the ways that people *use* their intelligence to learn. And Mary Meeker has moved us beyond remediation to actually assessing and strengthening learners' *ability* to learn. Building on their and others' work, we have the capacity to personalize both the process and the curriculum for every learner. We can develop a personal learning portrait and plan for people as individuals that incorporates what they know and how they learn as the starting points for further learning. Doing so is essential to successful learning.

Current knowledge about learning has outstripped the assumptions inherent in the traditional approach to education. The content of the curriculum can no longer be understood as fixed and static. Content cannot simply be accumulated and held by those who pursue formal education. From this point forward, when students graduate, most of the professions for which they have prepared will have standards and possibly structures that are different from those in place when they began their college educations. Knowledge—knowing content—is always important. In the current and projected environment, however, being able to think critically, reflect, adapt, and apply knowledge in multiple settings have become equally if not more important. The old proverb, "Teach a man to fish and he will eat for a lifetime," has never been more apt.

As we reach for the new education successes we need, we must grapple with the reality that every learner is distinctive in significant ways. One of the most important differences is the way each of us learns. If colleges teach two ways, and people learn eight or more ways, and every learner has a distinctive intellectual skills profile, why should we be surprised when the Law of Thirds asserts itself, failing one-third in high school and leaving one-third with only a high school diploma?

Teaching and learning can be organized such that they harness and direct the energy of the way each person learns naturally, converting it to more formal learning by connecting a known curriculum directly to the life of the learner. Just as surfers use the natural energy of waves for their rides, educators can use the natural energy of the instinct to learn to organize educational programs. As we look forward, we need a new architecture with different staffing, financing, and teaching models adapted to students' learning.

When universities fail students, too often the rationalization is, "They weren't ready for college." In fact, in too many cases, college was not ready for them. This die-hard tradition has to be changed if we are going to tap the hidden potential and knowledge in America's unserved learners.

5

Learning Is More Than
Strictly Academic

Millions of people have untapped knowledge and skills that go unrecognized by colleges and universities. As a result, they are ignored academically and in the workplace.

We have all seen the picture of two children with their noses pressed against a candy case. Boxes of candy and gum lie scant inches from them. But the children don't have the money to buy any.

We've also seen the image of a lonely person, looking from the street into a brightly lit room filled with comfort and friendship, where a family is gathered around the fire.

In such pictures, the thin pane of glass in the window separates two worlds as effectively as if it were a wall of fire. The people on the outside are left looking in at the objects of their desire, so near, yet so irretrievably far away.

These images are painful to imagine and difficult to accept. We commit time and effort in our local communities to breaking down the barriers they represent. But the picture of millions of adults being held back in life and in the labor market because colleges won't assess their learning in the workplace and from life for academic credit is just as disturbing. Having vast amounts of unrecognized knowledge is just as devastating to the American economy as having large pools of untapped potential.

As we approach the second decade of the twenty-first century, a practice as old as universities themselves continues to hold learners back. Colleges place high barriers between the learning that students have done outside of school and their progress toward the degree inside school. There are many arguments that justify this practice. One is, "You came here for what we can teach you." Another goes, "The program requirements just won't let us use your prior learning." At its root, however, the denial of experiential and other learning done outside of college is grounded in the concept that learning of value can only happen in academic settings.

According to the Educational Testing Service (ETS), we entered the twenty-first century forfeiting nearly a quarter of a trillion dollars every year as a result of our failure to educate Hispanics and African-Americans alone (Burn, 2002). These people are among the populations that are full of untapped potential and untapped knowledge, much of which is ignored or rejected by our traditional model of education.

Armed with knowledge and experience, personal learners are the Rodney Dangerfields of higher education. They just can't "get no respect." But, unlike Dangerfield's act, this is no joke. No matter what they actually know and can do, when learners cannot realize the value of their learning, they are separated from recognition in college and progress at work by the lack of validation of their still-hidden credentials. They are so near, yet so far away.

Personal learners bring knowledge with them, but most colleges ignore most or all of it, insisting on their own curricula as the only paths to a degree. Like the kids at the candy store, personal learners are left on the outside, knowing they have skills and abilities but unable to get at the credentials and rewards colleges have to offer.

There are three types of imprisonment resulting from this dangerous conceit. Learners are trapped academically, economically, and developmentally by their unrecognized learning. When we deny the value of experiential and other noncollegiate learning, we are stunting the learners' growth, assigning them different, lesser futures. And we are harming the longer-term economic health of the country.

When adult learners can't break out academically by getting their personal learning assessed for academic credit, they lose advantage and they also lose ground. College becomes more expensive, redundant, and time consuming as students take courses in areas that they have already mastered. Faced with soaring expenses, a longer time required to obtain a degree, and competing life priorities, millions of learners simply stop aspiring to attend college. For them, advanced academic and professional credentials are off-limits. Although they have the prerequisite learning and the developed capacity, they don't have the appropriate credentials to take higher-level courses.

As a result, unless they are extremely lucky or very entrepreneurial with assets to invest, they can't break out economically. Many adult learners simply stagnate, losing promotions as well as new career options. The more senior jobs that bring additional pay and better compensation are off-limits because they require additional credentials. Taking a different career path becomes impossible because the "transition" mechanism of further education is not available.

Beyond the academic and economic limitations that flow from unrecognized learning, there is a third type of imprisonment. We know that our lived experiences drive and shape the people we become, including the behaviors, skills, and attitudes that we have. But our lived experiences also shape how and what we learn successfully. Beyond our multiple intelligences, this cognitive capacity, formed by our lived autobiographies, influences the way we learn.

Allen Tough's research revealed that most people had forgotten the learning projects they had undertaken until he dredged them up through memory exercises (1971). In other words, we tend to forget not only *that* we learned but also *what* we learned.

Educators have long worried about the rate at which students actually forget what they have been taught and how to counteract that reality. It turns out that learning outside of the college walls has the same problem. We are continuously learning and changing, but we don't fully realize it, nor do we consciously retain the knowledge we acquire on a consistent basis.

If you do not develop the capacity to capture your learning, reflect on it, and turn it to your use, you can become a prisoner of your own experience. However, it turns out that being actively involved in the learning itself and actively reflecting on what has been learned are major factors in learning retention (Scheckley & Keeton, 2001). In this conception, a lifelong learner is someone who has developed the capacity to actively reflect on his or her learning throughout life, from all experiences, not someone who consumes courses and regurgitates content.

This, then, is one of the great challenges to our conception of higher education in the twenty-first century. If we are going to harness America's hidden talent and bring it to the economic and civic mainstream of the country, building on the personal learning of each individual is an essential component. Understanding the meaning of a learner's life experiences, including the more formal courses and workshops in which that individual participates, is an enormous educational opportunity for the learner and an equally significant professional opportunity for the educator. It can become the canvas on which we paint.

The educational value to the learner of assessing experiential learning goes far beyond the creation of a transcript where none existed before. I learned this reality first-hand at CCV. When we began assessing experiential and noncollegiate learning at the Community College of Vermont, I saw the evaluation of learning done outside of college in mechanistic terms, sort of like an academic audit of what a learner already knew. We did it because it was fair, the right thing to do, and practical. It was like recognizing advanced placement knowledge.

Soon, however, I learned firsthand that the process of assessing learning—actually distilling what has been learned and how and why—from the broad experience of life is far more than a valid way to get academic credit on a transcript. It is also deeply educational because it develops the learner's ability to reflect actively on his or her life experience, tickling out the learning from the totality of the experience. An early graduate of the Community College of Vermont captured this essential value of assessing life experience learning when she said, "Thanks for helping me see how much I have learned outside school, how much it was worth, and what kind of person I have become. Now I know I am a learner, and I'll never stop learning."

She was personalizing the value of active and focused reflection. Assessment of learning, done right, lies at the heart of education. It is the process through which learners understand what they know and how they learned it. In fact, the ability to reflect in a focused way is the flywheel of lifelong learning. For years, however, higher education has denied this personal learning. Without that assessment, and the reflection it requires, we are imprisoned by our own unreflected experience. When we deny the opportunity to assess and use this learning, moreover, we are stifling the renewable resource that nourishes America's talent, while simultaneously stunting the personal growth and development of adult learners.

The denial of personal learning has developmental as well as professional implications for personal learners. Gail Sheehy's *Passages* (1976) taught many of us about the transitions of age and development through which we move. As I considered the book, I was struck by how often the "passage" in question was experienced as a negative in life. I questioned myself then, "Are all developmental passages negative?"

Some calls to reflection are gentle: we go on vacation and read a book we have meant to read for years. Somehow, in the reading of it, we hear the call to introspection and change. Some calls to reflection are brutal: our child dashes into traffic and cannot be brought back to life. Or our loving mother is strangled by Alzheimer's before our eyes. Or we are called into our supervisor's office for coffee and told we are out of work. What evokes the call to reflect varies widely, not only among individuals but even within each of our lives. Once the reflection begins, however, it proceeds with a purpose.

I remember a day in the 1980s when I was sorting through old photographs. It was one of those lazy Sunday afternoon jobs saved for a winter weekend. I came across a picture of me, cradling one of my sons, taken at least a dozen years earlier, when I was at the Community College of Vermont.

As I looked at the smiling person holding the infant in the photo, I realized with a physical shock that I was looking at a stranger, a person who no longer existed. This was not the face that I saw in the mirror each morning when I shaved. This was someone much younger, insulated by his own naïveté, mostly uns- carred and unseasoned. This person had not known failure, had not suffered defeat. In the ensuing twelve years, I had become another person.

The intervening years had rushed by: my father's death, becom- ing a father for the third time, elections won and lost, and serving in statewide office. It was dizzying. There was a chasm of unre- flected experience between the man in the picture and the person I had become.

Looking at the stranger in the photograph, I realized that a river of unreflected learning and change had flowed by and over me. For whatever reasons—and there were many at play that Sunday after- noon, some glaringly public and others intensely personal—the shock of seeing myself as other than I was demanded my attention. I realized that I had grown away from the earlier version and become, for better or for worse, a new and different person.

Webster's dictionary says that reflection is the act of "careful consideration and the results thereof." Rita Weathersby, a devel- opmental theorist, claims that reflection is how we make meaning from experience. I am happy to draw on both definitions, thinking of reflection as the act or means through which we convert information and the raw material of experience into knowledge.

When we reflect on what we know and what we've experienced, we gain control over our lives, developing an understanding of what is happening, who we are becoming, and why. When we do not reflect in this way, we are flying blind, without any personal radar. We are living without the benefit of knowing the things that we have learned. We are living without the benefit of understanding the meaning in our life experience every day. We risk living our lives as victims of circumstance: unwitting prisoners of our own experience and learning.

My theory holds that there are times in a person's life when that individual updates the personally held image and understanding of who he is. That image, that person, is the person you see in the mirror every morning. But, after the update, life continues, giving you new experiences and new learning. As this new learning accumulates, the changes it encourages go largely unnoticed and unreflected. So, gradually yet ineluctably, you change, literally growing away from the person you were when you last took stock because of the experiences you are accumulating and their cumulative impact on you.

In this progression of events, there comes a moment when the new you, the becoming you, outweighs the older image, creating confusion and imbalance in your life. Then, almost always due to an external triggering event, you are forced into a crisis of rediscovery through reflection.

Tough's phrase "learning projects" sounds neat, nicely organized, and well packaged. In fact, our adult experiences with learning projects are ordinarily anything but tidy. We learn as we live, lurching from one thing to another, rarely achieving our goals on first attempts, learning as we go. Sometimes we learn as a way of coping with personal crises and changes. Often our most significant learning comes at untidy moments in our lives.

In addition to the untidiness, however, most of us haven't learned how to reflect consciously and seriously on the fact of our personal learning, let alone its value and impact on us. So, in many cases, learning is lodged in our lives as an iceberg of experience, revealing tips of knowledge. Through active reflection we can convert the raw material of experience to the more refined distillate of knowledge, achieving a finer alignment between our lived experiences and our conscious knowledge.

Martha, a divorced mother without a formal education or the credentials that go with it, saw her learning as a survival tactic. And she was very aware of the damage done to her life and career by her inability to convert her learning to a college context.

> Learning is a matter of survival. And it's important to know the worth of what you've learned. I've learned that I had done an awful lot in my life that I just didn't really think amounted to anything or served any particular purpose. People like me take a lot of what they already know, what they have, for granted. They think it is nothing, and they are wrong.
>
> As I have been going through the working world, I've found it very frustrating to have the knowledge to do a job, and yet because I did not have the degree, I was not able to get that job as far as having the title or getting the pay. You could get a person who would be fresh out of college that had the degree, and they would get the job having no experience. I would end up having to train them to do their job. This was an extremely frustrating spot to be in; I was not a degree holder so I did not qualify.
>
> I think a lot of people today that do not have degrees, but who do have common sense and working experience, have found out that wasn't what the employer was looking for. Employers put a high premium on the

degree these days. I myself would not only like to get an education, but I would also like to get ahead. And you have to have the formal degree if you're going to get anyplace.

To tell them that I sat in the library and read all these books on nuclear fusion or American history or whatever is not going to do a thing. But if I have gotten a grade from the professor, that will mean something.

Martha is caught on the outside by this academic conceit, held away from her full potential because her learning didn't happen in a college classroom. Standing right beside her is Ray.

Ray is a "shut out" from the system. As hard as our existing institutions work, and as successful as they are, there's no room for him there. Ray is a police officer in a small city outside of St. Louis. A solid man with a gruff demeanor, the first impression he gives is that of a cop. He, too, is learning from his experience and about himself. The respect he has earned among his fellow officers is reflected in his position as head of the Policeman's Association, but, as he approaches forty, Ray is less sure that he wants to continue doing police work for the rest of his life.

Eighty percent of the things I know about I learned on the streets. Those things don't fit directly into an institution of higher learning. But the biggest thing that a college could do for me is, when I sent my resume to somebody, I could write on there that I have these degrees, which I don't have now, and they would call me in for an interview. I am not the only one who feels that way. But is it going to be worth it to me to spend a lot of time on a traditional college education? I'm talking about me as an individual.

I know that if I can take that intelligence and integrate it into my reading, and then take the insight into

people that I have gained over all of these years, I probably know more about people than I do about anything
else. Honestly, if you could combine those things with
all the knowledge I have about how the world really is
and some other things I might have going for myself,
and my intelligence, then I've got pretty much what I
need. I know a lot, but I don't have the degree.

Ray knows a lot. He is aware of his learning and ready to take
advantage of opportunities to improve himself. His biggest obstacle
is the societal belief that learning only happens in school. As a
result, Ray can't have the knowledge, skills, and abilities that he
has attained at work recognized and validated by credits that can
be applied toward a degree.

Just as he is shut off by the tradition of higher education,
however, Ray is also blocked by business practice. Most business,
government, and nonprofit employers do not orient their recruit-
ing or promotion programs to seriously include personally learned
skills. So, people like Ray, lacking the stamp of approval from a
college or university, are out of luck.

Most people learn consciously throughout their lives. A hall-
mark of an educated person is the ability to reflect continuously
throughout life, making meaning from experience. Indeed, I
believe that lifelong learners are people who can consciously
extract meaning from the experiences they have.

And, as I first learned at the Community College of Vermont,
the value of assessing this learning goes far beyond getting credit
for it. The assessment itself is deeply educational, directly connecting the learners to their experiences, their changes, and their
development.

However, many learners are asked to return to school to attend
classes that duplicate the deep personal and life experiences they
already have in order to gain an "education." As the dean at
Harvard understood in my case, doing all this while continuing a

full-time job becomes a significant barrier to getting a degree for many.

Colleges are organized for eighteen-year-olds, young people without life experiences who really do not know very much. For them, the faculty has created a "stacked" curriculum. It moves from simpler to more complex items as the student "ages" in the schooling process.

People like Ray and Martha, with their experiences, learn differently and know more than the typical eighteen-year-old. But the hard reality is that even if they went back to school, neither Ray nor Martha would get much credit for the personal learning they had already done. In other words, they would start at the beginning, like eighteen-year-olds, and spend time and money to relearn things they already know, instead of getting advanced placement for that knowledge.

The bottom line is that if Ray and Martha don't play the game by the rules of the dangerous conceits, submitting to the limited menu that most colleges offer, the opportunities for which they are on alert will probably never arrive. And, when that happens, they will join the long line of wasted talent in America.

6

You Can't Get There from Here

I have had many classmates of mine drop like flies,
transfer from one college to the next, pay a truckload
of cash, and the end result is that not all of your credits
transfer. So you have to take the material that YOU
ALREADY KNOW all over. For what? I am currently
attending college in Medical Office Management, and I
want to transfer to another school when I graduate. They
told me that I have to take certain classes over because they
require them. Because of this, I now have to pick between
choosing another B.A. program or waste my money and
more importantly my time. I mean, if it's money that they
want, why don't they figure out some other way to scam
it out of us? But time, we cannot afford to waste.
(Shirley, rethinkinghighereduction.com, 2008)

You may have heard the old story about the traveler from "away" who loses his way on a back road in Maine. He pulls his shiny new Ford up beside an old farmer sitting at the side of the road on his equally old, beat-up John Deere tractor. The farmer is resting for a moment from mowing hay. The traveler, in a cheery voice, hails the farmer, "Which way to East Vassalboro?" The farmer, looking out from under his weather-beaten hat, thinks for a long moment and replies, "Well, son, you can't get there from here."

It's a wonderful story, which calls out the mythic Maine personality: laconic; terse; and with tongue-in-cheek, very dry humor. It's also just a bit of a put-down to people from "somewhere else" who always seem in a little too much of a hurry and have an air that suggests they probably know a great deal more than you. But, of course, the core proposition of the story, that "you can't get there from here," is preposterous.

Now, imagine that you are driving across the country to seek your fortune and make a life. Your plan is to get to California as soon as you reasonably can. But in West Virginia your car breaks down, costing you a few days as you get it repaired. And you stay a little longer than anticipated with some cousins in Des Moines because they needed help repairing their house. By the time you get to the Colorado border, you are pressing hard to finish the trip. After all, you need to get to the west coast and find a job!

But in Colorado there are agents at the border who stop your car. They note that you are running behind schedule and have made some unintended stops. So, as a penalty, they won't let you into Colorado until you back up five hundred miles and approach the border a second time. Then they wave you on through. It is arbitrary, unfair, and very frustrating. But there's nothing you can do about it.

Running low on money, you consider stopping in Denver and living there. But, ultimately, you push on. Then, the same thing happens at the Nevada border. You lose two more days, and California seems farther away than ever. And then again you are stopped in Needles, the desert entry point to California. Desperate and discouraged, you almost give up. But a little light flickers in your heart and you continue on. Nearly broke, however, you stop in eastern California and take the first job you can get, staying there three years before finally moving on to the coast.

If such a thing actually happened, you would be dumbfounded, then outraged. And properly so. In fact, you are probably thinking that the scenario is too far-fetched to take seriously. Think again.

This would never happen to you driving across the country. But, in yet another astonishing and dangerous conceit, higher education does exactly this type of thing to millions of students every year when it comes to the transfer of their academic credits.

More than half of today's college graduates attend two or more institutions on their journeys to the degree. That means they will, along the way, automatically be enrolled in a minimum of two different degree programs, even if those programs have the same name. Yet, most of our degree programs are written "from the bottom up," assuming that the students will be in the same college for their entire learning careers.

All students encounter a bewildering thicket of freshman requirements, general education requirements, prerequisites for majors, and then the majors themselves. Often, these are also embedded in other graduation requirements that must be satisfied before the degree is awarded.

So, every step of the way, students who switch programs at the same college or who transfer to new colleges pay a hidden "transfer tax," losing some of the academic credit they have earned at every turn. And, if they want to finish their trips, they need to enroll, pay again, and repeat the work. It is, truly, the college version of the trip to California. The route is well mapped if the trip goes smoothly. But if you get knocked off schedule for any reason, you have to go back five hundred miles at every border crossing.

As an antidote to this tendency, colleges have entered into articulation agreements to smooth the path for transferring students. But even these articulation agreements, often written between community colleges and their upper-division counterparts and offered as a solution to effective transfer, leak like an old boat when applied in real time:

- Sorry, the writing course at SkyPatch Community College just isn't good enough. We have standards here at Mesquite State. You'll have to repeat the course.

- No, we can't count the credit you earned at your "home college" while in the Serviceman's Opportunity College toward general education and prerequisites. It is better for you to complete those courses here with our faculty. Maybe you can squeeze some of it into your remaining elective courses.

- Yes, I know that you completed your general education requirements at Sasquatch State. But we have a different Gen Ed philosophy here, and half of your courses don't align with our standards. You'll need to do them again.

In fact, in a recent report issued by the Center on Reinventing Public Education, the authors found that "the presence of state-wide articulation and transfer agreements has not led to a significant increase in the number of community college students transferring to four-year institutions" (Gross & Goldhaber, 2009). The report went on to assert that this dangerous conceit has a disproportionate impact on learners from lower socioeconomic and minority ethnic backgrounds, the very people with whom we need to succeed. They concluded that "institutional factors" (that would be tradition) currently play a more important role in whether or not students actually transfer between sectors.

Just like when traveling the road to East Vassalboro, you can ultimately find your way in higher education. But the journey takes longer, is repetitive, costs you more, and postpones the plans that you have dreamed of achieving after you arrived.

Protecting academic standards is an old academic dodge to avoid engaging change. And, in the world of the horse-drawn plow, where few went to college and most people lived their lives within thirty miles of where they were born, it was unquestioned. Even today, if a person wants to change programs, or the licensure requirements change from state to state, going back and repeating work may be necessary, if expensive and frustrating.

Using the "not completed here" stamp to discount successful, perfectly legitimate learning completed elsewhere is, however, a travesty. And that stamp is used millions of times a year, prolonging the time and deepening the expense of attaining a bachelor's degree, and ending the educational journey entirely for millions of learners. It also consumes scarce federal and state financial aid dollars, while returning additional revenue to the treasuries of the institutions that deny the credit.

This old academic conceit has become a seething, current-day scandal. Many students give up. As Shirley said in the blog, they "drop like flies" or they "stop in Denver" and get jobs, ending their journeys. This explains, in part, why almost *forty million Americans* have some college credit, but not a degree. As you will see, there is an equally heavy financial price tag to go with the dreams deferred and job futures lost.

I first encountered this problem when I served as president of the Community College of Vermont (CCV). The college was accredited and part of the Vermont State Colleges system. But when our first graduates applied to one of the upper-division schools in the Vermont State College system, they were told they'd have to redo all their courses, because CCV was "outcomes based" and the courses wouldn't transfer.

Admitting that our transcript looked different, I did two things. First, I was able to negotiate a solution. Our graduates would be allowed to enroll and participate as juniors in the programs for which they had prepared. If they were successful academically, then we would work together with the senior institution to create a better translation of our credits to the receiving college's degree structure. If our graduates were not successful, then we would have to go back to the drawing board and redesign our program.

Because Vermont is a small state and we were able to frame the issue as whether or not our graduates could do the upper-level academic work successfully (the only issue that should matter), we broke the impasse. As I had hoped and believed, our graduates did very well, proving that success in college is not necessarily a function of taking the curriculum "from the bottom up."

Second, I developed an upper-division degree program, the external degree program, designed explicitly for returning adult learners. We then placed the program at one of the state colleges, where it operates to this day as a primary outlet for returning adults and community college graduates.

Today, we call this issue a lack of academic credit portability. Whether you switch programs within the same institution, transfer between institutions, or try to bring other learning into an institution from the military or corporate world, you will pay the "transfer tax," facing an almost certain discounting of the credits that you have already earned and paid for. AcademyOne, a company specializing in transfer effectiveness, estimates that the additional time and personal cost for most students is at least 15 percent, or between one and two extra terms (2008).

In addition to the inconvenience and expense borne by the students, the costs and the bureaucracy behind this issue are cumbersome and expensive for the institutions themselves and the government. There has been, however, little action taken to address the issue comprehensively, which would entail adapting a learner-centered focus, giving full credit for prior learning, and certifying the skills and knowledge that students bring with them.

This helps explain why, although federal student financial aid and veterans' education benefits have increased in dollars—as have enrollment rates at postsecondary institutions in recent history—the degree completion rate has not increased, and the country's rank internationally has declined in this area. We have millions of learners who decided to stop fighting the system.

Let's take a look at the students who hang on by their fingertips and actually fight their way through the system, pay for the redundancies and the setbacks, and get their degrees. In 2005, the General Accounting Office (GAO) released a study on transfer of college credit titled, *Transfer Students: Postsecondary Institutions*

Could Promote More Consistent Consideration of Coursework by Not Basing Determinations on Accreditation. The report confirms that we not only actively frustrate easy transfer and conversion of academic credit but also bear an extraordinary extra financial burden to sustain this "dangerous conceit."

The GAO report confirmed the following.

- Sixty percent of students attending a college or university will transfer at least once prior to receiving an undergraduate degree. This adds up to 2.5 million college students transferring each year.

- Although a majority of transfers occur within a state, approximately 35 percent of all transfers occur outside of the state of the institution in which the student first enrolled.

- Student transfers reflect a concept dubbed "swirling." This means that as well as occurring between two-year and four-year institutions, transfers frequently occur from four-year to four-year institutions, from four-year to two-year institutions, between programs within institutions, and from two-year to two-year institutions, as well as from public to private, public to public, and private to public institutions.

Here's how it hits the student. Swirling, coupled with institutional obstacles, requires that a student who wants to earn an undergraduate degree attend one additional semester at a minimum. In many cases, it requires an additional year in school or more.

But this is not where the damage stops. Because swirling is chaotic, not systematic, it increases

- student indebtedness;
- consumption of federal and state student aid;

- the cost of postsecondary education to students, institutions, and governments; and

- the time delay for students in joining the workforce and becoming taxpayers.

Swirling is costly to learners in terms of lost time. It reflects changes, disruption, and new circumstances in their lives. We know that it increases costs to them. But the overflow cost increase to all sectors of higher education and the government, as well as the economy, due to poor portability of credit is more than anyone might imagine.

AcademyOne, in an analysis of some of the costs resulting from the current processes used by institutions to transfer credit, found that:

- The annual costs for credits that do not help a student move toward a degree are estimated to exceed $7 *billion.*

- State subsidies reducing public costs for tuition and fees wastes nearly $14 *billion,* while reducing the institutions' capacities to serve more students and creating artificial demand.

- $5 *billion* of financial aid for credits taken and not counted toward an eventual degree are covered with student financial aid—which could be used so that more students are served.

- There are $6 *billion* in delayed tax revenue, because these students take at least an additional semester and often more to receive an undergraduate degree, delaying career advancement (2008).

So, for the students who make it, who actually proceed to a degree, the redundant costs for them, the institutions, and the governments involved approach $30 billion a year collectively.

In addition to the students who persevere, there are also some forty million people floating around in the system, with some credit and no credentials. As noted earlier, the Gates Foundation has argued that 50 percent of all annual expenditures, including financial aid, go for services to people who never receive a certificate or a degree (Wallis, 2008). These are the travelers who stopped in Denver, or Nevada, or Needles. They are a natural resource of enormous value, waiting to be discovered and recognized for the learning they have done and the capacities they exhibit every day. We need their knowledge and skills recognized in the workforce.

The lack of credit portability is an incalculable drag on our national goodwill. On top of the lost goodwill and duplicate costs, however, the lost income and tax revenue that these travelers represent is significant. Although a precise calculation is extremely difficult, if we use the estimates provided by the Bureau of Labor Standards, the difference between a high school graduate and a baccalaureate degree holder is over $20 thousand a year and growing (Jones, 2009). Using that number, for every one million Americans caught in this trap, the annual impact is $20 billion! The numbers, and the lost tax revenue, not to mention productivity, add up pretty quickly.

As bad as all this news is for personal learners, it is just as bad that our inability to make academic credit earned from accredited colleges truly portable presents a clear and present danger to America's economic stability. Without portability, merit is meaningless.

What should we do about this old and dangerous conceit? There is a strong reluctance among postsecondary education institutions, education systems, and even some states to address how academic credit portability could be managed by systematic methods outside their total control. Doing this would require a commitment to design programs and courses aligned with the reality of what learners need—a means to transition between programs and locations over time without huge penalties and costs imposed by institutions protecting curriculum that was designed to be self-contained.

Currently, postsecondary education institutions are limited by their policies, practices, and lack of automation. In addition, most institutions have not adjusted to the new enrollment patterns, the "swirling" of millions of students a year. Some institutions have negotiated individual articulation agreements with other institutions. Some states have created articulation agreements, and a few states have developed common course numbering systems to support credit portability. For example, the New Mexico legislature mandated a common course numbering system for most freshman and sophomore courses at the state's public institutions. This will facilitate transfer of credit within the state.

These steps alone, however, will not solve the problem. There is no systematic way of creating, maintaining, and displaying course equivalencies at a national level with one authoritative source. As a result, it is very difficult for either students or institutions to navigate the postsecondary education system during the transfer process.

A simple analogy helps describe what can be established. Imagine an academic credit portability system that works like the E-Z Pass toll system, which has been instituted in some parts of the northeastern highway system, including New Jersey, New York, and Pennsylvania. An academic credit portability system designed to help students navigate their academic journeys would work across state and institutional boundaries, just like traveling by car with one electronic record for the collection of tolls. Thus the states and institutions would be adopting a common transport and standardized delivery of services that would address the issue of students' mobility in their efforts to gain credentials and degrees.

The real need is to find a way to create a system that addresses course equivalencies, whether or not one has received a degree. That will enable the student to change colleges, secure in the knowledge that the credits already earned at one institution will not be discounted by the receiving institution, thus hampering his or her progress toward meeting degree credit requirements.

Such a system must respect and support academic freedom. Course equivalencies need to be determined by institutions and their faculty. By creating such a system, however, the level of student indebtedness can be reduced, costs of a degree to the state and the student will be lower, and the chances these students will enter the workforce sooner and become taxpayers will increase.

Basically, it is necessary to do the following.

- Improve the management and quality of postsecondary data for the administration of the transfer of credits.

- Create agreements among institutions that enable the streamlining of the transfer process.

- Establish a national course database and curriculum information system in higher education.

- Automate the processing and evaluation of transfer of earned student credits.

- Facilitate the creation of an electronic system across states that keeps current course equivalencies, enabling the efficient and speedy transfer of earned student college credits (AcademyOne, 2008).

We should have two goals. First, we need to eliminate or reduce the "transfer tax" on students that stems from increased fees, costs, and time spent as a result of being forced to take redundant courses when moving from one institution to another. Second, we should reduce significantly the increased costs that this redundancy imposes on state and federal budgets that finance participation in higher education.

Universities throughout Europe have begun to move in this direction through a negotiated understanding called the Bologna Process. The process offers enhanced transparency and portability to the sixteen million students studying in the European Union countries involved. The Bologna Process is responsible, among other things, for the design and implementation of a common course evaluation architecture based on learning outcomes. Coupled with other agreements on degree structure and common understandings of progress to the degree, the consistent course architecture provides far greater latitude for participating students. We should find ways to achieve the same outcome here.

Institutions and state systems of higher education must use a more sophisticated approach to assist students in managing the transfer of credit and making the process fairer, more efficient, and more accurate. Nero earned his place in history by fiddling while Rome burned. Will America continue to dither while students are denied credit when transferring between colleges; while successful learners, already in the workforce, are denied the true value of their earned credit; and, as a result, while the country is weakened?

As we will see in Part Three, "From Access to Success: A New Ecology of Learning," we have the resources available today, the capacity, to bring millions of learners to the economic mainstream if we decide to do it. To do this, however, we need first to understand what we face and get beyond two enormous obstacles: the dangerous conceits of higher education and the resulting lack of sufficiently educated workers.

Having fewer workers with the necessary education and skills than we have available jobs requiring those skills turns the assumptions and logic that have driven our education and employment systems upside down. In the old days, lack of merit was a disqualifier, used to winnow out some so that others would get the scarcer high-skilled jobs. Today, however, merit is a qualification we must achieve in many more people, so they can take the jobs being created and learn the changes in job structure, skill sets, and requirements that will certainly arise in the years ahead.

Part III

From Access to Success: A New Ecology of Learning

We have a country in which there are millions of personal learners with high school educations and maybe some college. We know that many of them are capable people who have continued to learn as they make their ways through life. And we know that our education and credentialing systems are uneven and poorly articulated, frustrating the recognition of the learning these individuals have accomplished in regard to both the awarding and the transfer of credit. Added to this continuously renewing, self-generating intellectual and behavioral turmoil is the historic change in our workforce needs. For the first time, there are more high-skill jobs than there are people with sufficient training and education to fill them. And, if we don't figure out how to tap the wasted talent American adults already possess, we will fall further behind in the global economic sweepstakes.

Colleges and universities appear to be "maxed out" when it comes to solving this problem. On the one hand, they are trapped by the economics of a mature operating model that reflects the best of academic tradition. They do their job well, and we need them to keep doing it. On the other hand, the economics of the model prohibit its continued, rapid expansion. At the same time, beyond economics, these educational institutions have practices that compound their inflexibility, adding to their inability to meet the emerging needs. These "dangerous conceits" frustrate the natural relationships of the emerging ecology of learning.

Now, however, we have reached a tipping point. The "learning possibility" has moved beyond making time- and place-bound "access" available on campuses and in the evenings. The increasing capacity of the World Wide Web has revolutionized our ability to manage learning and assessment. That capacity, coupled with our ability to better harness the knowledge we have about how people learn, creates an enormous opportunity for many people to move beyond access to success. Today, they can access curricular content freely, riding the Long Tail of education. Adult learners will be able to use new services that customize learning to their needs anywhere, anytime. This is our "new ecology" for higher education.

Chapter Seven, "The End of Scarcity: Education's Emerging Long Tail," describes the reality of abundant information and its growing impact on learning and education. It presents the proposition that the web and the resulting Long Tail of education change everything. As the blog The Technium (2008) has written, when virtually all information is available, accessible, and reproducible for free, the value that the institution adds to the education-learning equation must change. The explosion of information capacity inherent in Web 2.0 creates the ability to bring those who have historically been on the margins of education to the main-stream of opportunity. It will effectively end scarcity and, with it, the historic control of a dominant, traditional educational model.

Chapter Seven identifies and discusses the end of scarcity in higher education content and access and the impact of this emerging abundance on higher education as we know it today. It expands on earlier discussions about personalization and how people learn best in the developing era of abundance. Finally, it describes the additional great value of information technology in assuring academic quality through clearly measured learning outcomes, consistent standards, and reliability of assessment.

Then, as you will read in Chapter Eight, "Game Changers: New Media and the Open Education Resource Movement," Web 2.0 has flipped the historic assumptions about the organization and delivery of higher education upside down, bringing first-rate, high-quality learning resources within the reach of every person. Although the enduring and practical problem of the digital divide still hamstrings learners everywhere, this chapter describes the potential that technology in its multiple forms and applications has for changing the learning paradigm.

"Game Changers" describes how the gap between what is possible in learning and what institutions of education are actually doing is widening significantly. Furthermore, it makes the link between the potential that information technology brings and Clayton Christiansen's (2008) concept of "disruptive technology," describing their impact on the dominant model of education. It includes a discussion of exemplar events and projects, which, collectively, frame the emerging technologically enhanced environment and its potential for the reorganization of the educational equation—a new ecology.

After touching on the "one laptop for every child" effort sponsored by Nicholas Negroponte as an exemplar of the spread of access to technology and the consequences of that access, Chapter Eight also discusses the Open Education Resource (OER) movement, including the Global OpenCourseWare Consortium initiated by MIT. This floodtide of high-quality technology and course materials into the open resource space will permanently mark a new balance between content, the learner, and recognized learning. The development of iTunes U and wiki-university is further evidence of this movement.

All of these resources will, in turn, reshape education toward personalization and adaptation. The chapter closes with a discussion about new ways to assess learning, including simulations and games. In this emerging world, attending a campus will, for a majority of learners, evolve from being essential to being preferred, to being a choice among other choices when it comes to getting an accredited college degree.

Chapter Nine, "Reaching the Middle Third: Talent-Friendly Colleges for the Twenty-First Century (C21Cs)," describes new institutional forms and policies that begin to define the constitution of these new entities. They will dramatically change the relationship between learners, learning, and colleges in a massive redesign of the educational value proposition, establishing a new learning marketplace.

"Reaching the Middle Third" describes the elements of a paradigm that uses information-age tools to capitalize on the capacity of every learner, personalizing education to meet their needs. In order to compete globally, we need to renew our intellectual infrastructure and develop our workforce by doing what America does best: reinventing and redefining the value proposition for education based on what we know and our best analysis of future needs. The chapter includes program and policy designs, which, implemented well, will break the Law of Thirds and create the workforce and learning force that America needs for the twenty-first century.

The conclusion, "A New Ecology of Learning," draws the arguments together and points them toward the future. If we fail to understand this new ecology of learning, we are in the path of a perfect storm of failure in terms of education, access, and economic stability. And our penalty, beyond failing to seize the opportunity to serve the workforce and meet the economic, social, and civic needs of our society, will be that the traditional system of higher education will become less relevant to the future. We will be failing ourselves as well as the country's needs.

If, however, we can harness the natural power of this new ecology and understand its rhythms and ways, we can sail through the storm to a sunny future, in which new approaches to higher education operate alongside the existing system, as parts of a new ecology in the higher education world. We must move to embrace this new ecology of learning and the social, civic, and economic success that it will generate.

7

The End of Scarcity
Education's Emerging Long Tail

Ed was frustrated and pensive. For the third time in three years, he had been passed over for a job promotion that he knew he could handle. As he left the HR office with the bad news, it finally began to sink in. Even with his learning from the army and a year at the local community college, his college record didn't add up to a degree. And it took a degree to qualify for the position. As he drove home, he felt as if he were in a straitjacket, but that it was made of gauze. He could move, but he couldn't go anywhere. He thought angrily, "That college is right down the road from where I work. I drive past it every morning on my way in and every night on my way out. And yet it might as well be a million miles away! That's no 'shining city on a hill,' that's a castle with the drawbridge pulled up. But what else can I do?"

Higher education's greatest strength, as it has been designed, built, and developed, is a great weakness when it comes to addressing the needs facing America today. Although we have redefined and extended higher education opportunities dramatically over the last sixty years, our system of higher education is based on and organized around the principle of scarcity, that the resources needed to provide an education must be collected in one place—a campus—because there is an insufficient supply of those resources in the general community. Not enough faculty members. Not enough classrooms. Not enough laboratories. Not enough library books. There was no other way to "do" higher education. And, on the outside, there was a scarcity of jobs requiring more than a high school education, creating the need for a meritocracy to decide who would compete for them.

Organizing scarce community resources to create valuable institutions—colleges and universities—has served us well, creating educational opportunities while building research centers and professional education programs of unparalleled quality and depth. In fact, there was no other choice. Scarcity was a reality in the world of information, teaching, and learning until the early 1990s, when the Web was born. Essentially, the principle of scarcity says that for an institution to be valuable to the community around it, it must offer a service that community members can't get more cheaply or with higher quality somewhere else. The scarcity, based on an inability to duplicate the resource, controls the market.

Colleges are built around the curriculum. They organize facilities, faculty, libraries, and laboratories (not to mention gorgeous dorms and playing fields) to host, support, and entertain the students who come to learn. They compete for students and market to students based on the quality of the living and learning experience offered by the campus. And faculty members are paid to teach, assist in the governance, and do research. Finally, as we know all too well, there is a funding and spatial limit to the number of students who can attend at any one time.

As a scarce commodity, access to college has traditionally favored people who had time for college, could afford college, and could learn effectively in colleges as they were structured. Scarcity created a standard for access that favored some learners over others who learned differently, had to work, or were constrained by other social and economic forces. For years, such incentives as student financial aid were provided to generate more access for those who had been marginalized. There was, however, no alternative to the traditional model and its campuses. Today, stalled by diminishing returns and soaring costs, and surrounded by information abundance, traditionally organized institutions are no longer the only source of solutions.

Historically, prestige and quality in higher education have been determined as much by who is denied as by who is accepted. Quality has subtly become a replacement for "scarcity," converting it to a virtue. We all know the argument: "Of course we don't take everyone who applies, we have standards." By implication, those who have not been admitted are less qualified and capable than those who have been admitted. That works for institutions that are filled with students who fit their molds. And it works in societies in which there are a limited number of "knowledge-based" jobs. But it doesn't work for the capable learners who are left on the outside or for the larger society with significant vacancy rates in many high-skill jobs.

As successful as higher education has been in so many ways, this natural scarcity has generated parallel perverse effects. It has become part of our cultural mythology that says, "There is a reason for this scarcity of opportunity. Opportunity is not for you. It's for the 'smart' people, those who can benefit from college." Listen to Bob as he describes his emotional reaction when he finally went to college. He was sure that he would be "dumb" in school.

> So, I finally dragged myself over to the community college and took two courses. And I was scared to death. I had been at war, in police riots, and a firefighter and that was all right. But now I'm going to this college and I'm scared to death. I literally had stomach cramps—got physically sick. I really don't know why I was scared. I had no idea … no reason … it had nothing to do with anything … there was no consequence to pay. There was no overt, physical, explicit consequence. I could

have gone there, flunked out, and nothing would have happened. I still would have been a lieutenant in the fire department. Nothing would have changed.

I was sold this bill of goods about college, that everyone who graduated from college was far superior to the average guy walking the street. I don't say it's a conspiracy, but I think at some level people actually peddle that attitude to keep some people out of colleges and some people in them. Where I come from, it's meant to keep them out because there's only so much room at the top. It's that simple.

Bob is describing, up close and personal, what it is like to look at the scarcity equation from the outside. In addition to the rules and policies that are unfriendly to adult learners and their talents, the tradition of scarcity itself can crush hope and aspiration, giving capable people reasons to not even try.

The principle of scarcity was still applying itself as it almost defeated Bob. Since the end of World War II and the implementation of the GI Bill, America has done an extraordinary job in building new campuses and making those campuses more accessible with loans and grants. In the last thirty years, however, that extraordinary superstructure of higher education has become more costly in terms of both deferred maintenance and the cost of doing business more generally. So, costs are up while appropriations for institutional support are down.

The Law of Thirds and its manifestation, the success ceiling, are driven by limited access and academic models and policies unfriendly to many learners and much learning. Now, however, in Bob's words, there is more "room at the top." We need to expand opportunity to create a more educated workforce to fill the jobs of the future. But the model simply is not sufficient. The "scarcity" model leaves out capable people who, for whatever set of reasons, find themselves on the margins of social, economic, and educational activity, struggling to get a seat at the American table of opportunity. They are victims of the Law of Thirds. More of the same cannot be tolerated in this new environment.

As we saw in "Wasted Talent," our national well-being depends on our creating much more success through postsecondary education. We must break through the success ceiling, rewrite the Law of Thirds, and encourage many more people to attain greater levels of educational achievement. Failing to provide access and the serious prospect of success in higher education and advanced workforce positions to two-thirds of our population is socially, civically, and economically untenable. A population that can't provide for itself is a population deprived of the basic American promise: hope for a better future. American learners need the learning they deserve, and the recognition of their capacities that they have earned. America needs a civic force and workforce ready for the twenty-first century.

Happily, the story of American higher education policy has been an unfolding drama of assaults on the dominant form of scarcity of the day or the period. Each time, as new people came to learning, or lay leaders saw a new need that higher education was not meeting and would not meet, the forces of order argued that the change in standards would be fatal to the quality inherent in the established order, one way or the other. And each time they have been proved wrong by newly powerful people who graduated and entered the social, civic, and economic life of the country, changing the society for the better. It hasn't always been pretty, but it has worked.

Today, once again, we are faced with a significant challenge to improve and recognize the learning that millions of Americans do. This time, however, conditions in society, beyond our campuses, are aligning to create an abundance of learning opportunities, using new tools and knowledge to change the rules, reinterpret the higher education world, and win the battle. There are three big changes, unleashed by technology and the global economy, which affect education. They eliminate scarcity as we have experienced it, creating a new ecology of learning that will drive successful change.

A Future of Unlimited Content

Our capacity to meet the critical need for more highly skilled and educated Americans has changed dramatically. The technology revolution, still in its early stages, is standing the historic organizing ethic of higher education—scarcity—on its head more powerfully than the Morrill Land Grant Act, the GI Bill, the rise of community colleges, the Civil Rights Act of 1964, and the Pell-Stafford financial aid revolution, all taken together. The Open Education Resource (OER) movement, iTunes U, and the Global OpenCourseWare Consortium have opened an era in which excellent, organized curricula are at the fingertips of every potential learner. Technology is obliterating the old boundaries defined by the campus and its schedule, leaving multiple possibilities to provide organized learning opportunities. Even as it creates other challenges, a content-rich world, accessible and diverse, is developing more rapidly every day. Technology, coupled with the skill and knowledge demands driven by globalization, put curricular scarcity out of business, transforming higher education by radically changing both the profile of the demand and the characteristics of the supply.

In October 2008, almost one million people hit the Web site of the MIT OpenCourseWare initiative to download at least one course. Introduced several years prior, MIT's radical innovation has placed the university's entire curriculum online for public use without any cost to the user. Five years later, many of the users were faculty and students from MIT and other colleges and high schools, just as MIT had expected. But, as a big and continuing surprise to everyone involved in this extraordinary project, half of the users were not faculty or students from other colleges and universities. They were self-described self-learners (MIT/OCW, 2008).

Think about it. In one month, more than half a million people in the United States downloaded one or more courses from one of the premier universities in the world, *for purely personal purposes*. Put another way, personal learning projects, each person's innate capacity and instinct to learn, first identified and labeled by Allen Tough over forty years ago, met the Internet in a way that could be measured. This content, however, beyond raw life experience or workplace-based training modules, is the curriculum of a major, world-class research university. The doors to the informal consumption of a college curriculum on a broad scale, closed for so long, have been opened.

When I heard this news, another door, long closed so securely that I never questioned it, opened in my mind. The content of a college curriculum, the stuff and substance of which it is composed, is no longer a scarce commodity. The activity of these self-described self-learners and the availability of the MIT curriculum symbolize the end of scarcity for college curricula specifically and organized knowledge generally.

In revolutionary America, Benjamin Franklin conceived of the public library, calling it "the university of the common man." When the Community College of Vermont, Empire State College, and several other noncampus colleges were founded in the 1970s, they represented a philosophical statement and commitment to take learning to the learners in off-campus settings and respond to the needs of the learners. In the "scarcity" environment of the 1970s and 1980s, however, these innovative institutions were still organized as political and educational alternatives to the campus model, employing new versions of the dominant teaching-learning approach. Now, in a startling and revolutionary extension of that vision, you can get what you want, when you want it, for your own personal learning and pleasure. It is at your fingertips, customized with search engines for the needs or interests that you have.

In his breakthrough book *The Long Tail*, Chris Anderson (2006) provides an explanation for this previously implicit but powerful aspect of the Web. Using the music and book publishing industries as examples, Anderson describes the mobility of information as well as the low cost of its storage as new drivers of a world in which any person can get any piece of information at any time for pretty low prices.

Gone are the days when a product had to be popular in order to be available—when inventory decisions, driven by projected sales, determined the availability of a book or a CD. Gone are the days when "king-maker" experts, supported by scarcity, determined which songs were popular and which were not.

Education's Long Tail does the same thing for curriculum content. We are entering an age in which more people, using fewer resources per person, will have access to a previously unimaginable variety of information resources. And, just as with iTunes U, previously excluded people will be able to get the exact information they want, when they want it.

> Penny smiled as she thought about the whole scenario. Who would have thought that a casual inquiry about how people behaved would lead to this? She had seen an article about the customs of immigrants and their struggle to find a balance between their traditions and the pressures of living in a new society. As she had googled related issues, she found herself immersed in readings about culture and anthropology, with video clips and lectures available through links. And that, in turn, had led to conversations and readings about organization culture, how people behaved in the workplace. Now, she was heading back to school, primarily online, so that she could keep her job and finally get her Bachelor of Professional Studies degree, with an emphasis on how organizations work best. Even better, the

learning outcomes for her program of studies were linked not only to graduation requirements but also to the industry-related management requirements she would need to satisfy if she wanted a promotion. Talk about two for the price of one!

People who want a higher education, especially those who have not had access to one, will have new choices. Policymakers looking for a way to bring millions of Americans from the margin of economic opportunity to the mainstream of social and civic life have new choices as well. We need an additional, entirely different set of educational approaches if we are going to successfully harness the potential of education's emerging Long Tail, thus satisfying the critical national need for a bigger, more educated workforce to meet the demands of the emerging global economy.

Mark Hopkins, the renowned philosopher and educator, introduced the concept of "sitting on a log" with a student, discussing knowledge. This extension of the Socratic dialogue, long held as one of the finest ways for teaching and learning to happen, is now possible directly and indirectly, anytime, anywhere, with a mentor or a teacher, formally or informally. The growing availability of high-quality curricular content can provide previously unserved learners with online, blended, and face-to-face opportunities for high-quality teaching and learning that have not existed before. We have returned to one of the taproots of western culture, a historic foundation for teaching and learning, the one-to-one conversation, only to discover a previously unimaginable future.

Oxford University has been considered one of the finest universities in the history of the world. Among other reasons, this stature has been conferred because students at Oxford are encouraged to read and be in dialogue with their professors in a focused, yet open, search for answers. With education's Long Tail in play, we are now entering an age in which Mark Hopkins's log is electronic and a simulation of the Oxford approach can be achieved @.edu.

The end of content scarcity changes forever the relationship between colleges and the learners who seek the education and credentials they offer. As surely as spring follows winter, people will become increasingly comfortable with choices that are available, accessible, and cheap when it comes to pursuing learning outside of colleges' traditional instructional format.

Imagine Allen Tough's adult learning projects with boundless additional amounts of prepackaged information to support the learning. But, as we already know, when people learn something, they want to get formal recognition for their learning. This instinct, to be recognized with academic credit for what they know and can do, is forming a rising tide of aspiration in millions of learners, which laps up against the walls of the ivory towers at our institutions of learning. The world, and the relationship between the learner and the university, is changing, driven by Web 2.0.

A Future of Unlimited Access

Physical scarcity has driven the educational equation since the first itinerant monk walked rural Europe in the 1400s, carrying a book from which he read. Resources available to educate people, compared to the need, have always been scarce. Too few books, too few faculty members, too few campuses, too few libraries and laboratories. Campuses reflect the same scarcity through their physical limitations and their funding formulas. Access is limited.

As the British Open University (BOU) has shown for over thirty years, however, the size of the student body does not have to be controlled by available classroom space, faculty, or other resources that are available in the campus setting. Knowledge about how people learn coupled with the capacity of Web 2.0 create a high-potential learning environment in which rich curricular materials, combined with highly personalized support and adaptation, can be delivered to capable but previously excluded learners. Degree-level services can be delivered anytime, anywhere, to anyone.

We face an unprecedented situation. College campuses, organized around the principle of physical scarcity, were built on the assumption that the campus was necessary to the overall endeavor of learning. However, they now exist in a world in which there are no physical barriers to learning. The only actual barriers to access are capacity to do the work and ability to pay. Libraries are still important, but learners have access to previously unimaginable intellectual resources to support their learning from a wide and expanding universe of sources.

In this environment, an increasing number of learners are ahead of the colleges and their faculties. These learners understand and are using the technology and content available. It is the colleges that are trapped by their economics and their cultures, unable to maximize the new tools available. This is one of the reasons why, as we have discussed earlier, the ability of higher education to increase its success rate has stalled. It appears that the entire sector has hit its success ceiling, like an interstate highway system built for the 1970s that is paralyzed with traffic congestion in the early twenty-first century.

All this is happening at a time when we need to bring additional millions of capable learners from the margins of our society to the mainstream of economic opportunity. We don't want, or need, less higher education access. We need more. Abundant access is our friend.

A Future with Abundant High-Skill Jobs

The workplace demand for educated people with at least an associate's degree has reversed itself. For the first time in our history, we have more jobs requiring higher-order learning and education than we have people to fill them. In fact, a survey of the 175 fastest growing occupations in 2008 revealed that most of them required at least an associate's degree, with many preferring the bachelor's or higher (Bureau of Labor Statistics, 2008). We can no longer assume a scarcity of need for educated people. We must organize for abundance, generating every trained and educated person we can get.

This remained true even during the downturn in 2008–2009, when jobs requiring specific skills (for example, nursing) remained unfilled even as the unemployment rate was rising. This is a complete reversal of employment life as we have known it. Let's revisit some of the facts.

- Growth in the number of working Americans has slowed as population growth has slowed.

- As our population ages, the percentage of people in the workforce is declining.

- Twenty-five- to thirty-four-year-olds have a lower high school graduation rate than did older Americans.

- By 2014, 78 percent of all jobs will require some postsecondary education.

- Only 35 percent of Americans have at least an associate's degree.

- There will be a skilled labor shortage of seven million jobs by 2010 and twenty-one million jobs by 2020 (Jones, 2009)

The entire higher education system has been built around the assumption that there are fewer jobs that require a college education than there are people to fill them. Indeed, as I discussed earlier, the very concept of "meritocracy," the Jeffersonian principle that underlies so much of our American promise, assumes that getting the "good" jobs should be based on merit. That makes sense. But what happens if there are more "good" jobs than there are people to fill them? The answer, from a domestic policy perspective, is "nothing good."

In this emerging marketplace, our education system needs to be creating and validating merit. We need to figure out how to recognize capacity in all its forms, not screen it out. Pat Callan, president of the National Center for Public Policy and Higher Education, addressed the issues of cost and diminishing returns as he explained the center's 2008 report: "When we come out of the recession, we're really going to be in jeopardy, because the educational gap between our workforce and the rest of the world will make it very hard to be competitive. Already, we are one of the few countries where 25- to 34-year-olds are less educated than older workers."

Obstacles to Adoption

The scarcity assumption has become artificial. No longer representing an unchangeable reality, scarcity of resources currently describes a choice, a consequence of history, not a contemporary necessity. Colleges' and universities' models of operation come from a different time, a time when you had to ride your horse across town to see if your friend was home to chat.

Unfortunately, two additional factors complicate our adoption of the necessary changes in how we think about higher education. First, as individuals and as a society, we can be slow to recognize, grasp, and accept large-scale changes that come at us like this. The significance of the end of scarcity, and the consequences that follow on its heels, are either denied or misunderstood by many, both inside and outside of education. We like our traditions because they are familiar, a means of understanding the world around us. They give us comfort and organize our world.

Second, as a consequence, the technology driving abundant information is underutilized in higher education, while some of its implications are ignored because they challenge many traditions.

As things currently stand, technology is, more often than not, integrated with the curriculum and the organization of the university as it has historically been organized. For example, podcasts of lectures are available for the learners. They are also used to maximize convenience, getting students quicker, up-to-date information about events on campus.

These uses tinker at the margins of the traditional educational model. More fundamental questions might include:

- How might an institution integrate Google, the Global OpenCourseWare Consortium, or iTunes U into the base of its approaches to curriculum, teaching, and learning?
- Can we get beyond the semester structure to a non-time-based approach?
- Can we educate people in asynchronous formats?
- Can we guarantee the reliability and consistency of the learning we recognize? Or will the evaluation of learning remain the personal interpretation of an individual faculty member?

Earlier, I noted the irony of the fact that the very universities that created the science that describes how and why people learn then failed to incorporate that knowledge into their approaches to teaching and learning. Again the irony raises its head. Higher education is not able to respond to the deep implications of these revolutionary changes, many of which were incubated in their own research labs and graduate schools.

American history is filled with stories about underutilizing new technologies in their early years, of failing to grasp their significance in its full dimension. One possibly apocryphal example can be drawn from the early years of the telephone. People would call their friends across town.

"Jack, are you home today?"

"Sure, Pete, all day."

"Great, I'll be right over to talk."

Pete would then go over to Jack's house, secure in the knowledge that his friend would be there when he arrived. Of course, there's always the chance that Jack and Pete knew the town telephone operator would be listening in and didn't want to share their conversation with the world.

But it is more likely that Pete saw the phone as the best means of making sure Jack was there. What could be better than knowing for sure that Jack would be at home? It reduced all the risk of wasted time and guaranteed a good conversation. Now that's a step ahead!

Or, to bring the point closer to home, how about uses of the cell phone? It's a terrific improvement on the telephone, and receiving e-mail and having Web access make it even more useful. My grown children, and my younger colleagues, use the cell phone as a comprehensive communications device, with Facebook as a new form of a very old idea, the town commons.

On my last birthday, I received dozens of "Happy Birthdays" from friends, family, and colleagues. As happy as it made me, it was unexpected. Finally, I asked one of the well wishers, "How did you remember it was my birthday?" She replied, "It's on my Facebook homepage, because you're my friend." I cannot imagine how thirteen-year-olds are using these devices to learn, let alone the adults of the future.

These are two little examples of a principle that is replayed again and again during the change process. As a cell phone user, I am culturally influenced by the patterns of usage I understand. I miss the larger implication of the phone because I can't see through the immediate adaptation—way better phone access and e-mail services—to imagine far more profound potential uses, including as a communication center and an electronic town commons.

Like Pete and Jack, and many of the rest of us, most colleges have held the information revolution and the technology that supports it at arm's length, considering them as academic enhancements, if at all. They have asked the question, How does it help us do what we do, only better? As a result, the major breakthroughs to date have not been in new learning design and assessment or in portability. They have concerned access to education, getting material to people who couldn't get it before. Although this is important, it is a gross underutilization of technology's educational potential.

Thomas Kuhn described this tendency at length in *The Structure of Scientific Revolutions* (1962). He describes a cycle of acceptance of new ideas that begins with rejection of the new, evolves into tolerance, and ultimately shifts to embrace and acceptance. Whether it was Aristotle's teachings, Newton's physics, or the iMac, the first instinct of tradition is to repel new thoughts that rest on different assumptions. Then, as experience with the new thoughts (some might call it data) is accumulated, tradition accommodates and ultimately is transformed by the emerging knowledge.

As we have discussed earlier, our system of higher education is excellent. American colleges and universities educated more than fifteen million students in 2006. But we need many more graduates, not fewer. America's emerging and mounting needs for the future are an entirely different story. If we rely on these same campuses to take responsibility for doubling the number of associate's and bachelor's degree holders by 2025, we will fail. Here are a few reasons why this is so.

- We would need to double our higher education capacity, doubling also the number of associate's degree holders. I know of no political equation that anticipates the financing of people and property necessary to double our current campus capacity.

Campuses are stretched thin today, straining to maintain the facilities that they have. State and federal coffers, already burdened by exploding program and infrastructure costs coupled with lagging revenues, are struggling to sustain funding for existing programs of all kinds. Government financial support for higher education institutions, adjusted for inflation, is trending level or down, whereas financial support for individual students is trending up.

- To double our graduation numbers using the existing higher education model, we would need to dramatically increase the number of faculty members teaching in our universities. I see no political calculus that would successfully garner the funds necessary to train and employ them. But the demand for top people in the science, technology, engineering, math, and language areas outside of higher education will also defeat this goal. People with the necessary qualifications can make significantly more money working outside the academy. I see no analysis that suggests this reality will change for the better, favoring traditional higher education. So, even if we could afford to increase our capacity by 50 to 75 percent, there will not be a sufficient, qualified workforce available in the traditional format to fill the needed positions.

- Finally, colleges will have their hands full just achieving a higher student success rate with the spaces and facilities they have. Current trends suggest that, as tuition is increased to offset budget decreases from other sources, the amount of money actually going to instruction and student support will decline. The law of diminishing returns suggests that future improvements in the success rates will be marginal in relation to the problem that needs to be solved. So, although Bob DePrato finally made his way into college, millions of other learners will remain on the outside, looking in.

The requirement for our existing colleges and universities is clear. We need our traditional system of higher education to continue as it is, with continuing improvement, to hold the center of the spectrum and sustain America's educational greatness in its historical format. To some people, it may seem ironic. But, as successful as our traditional higher education model has become, what got us where we are won't get us where we need to go.

We also need a dramatic new vision for the future, with new types of organizations and institutions to achieve the increased academic success required to survive. This reformulation of how we offer higher education is now possible. Web 2.0 is making the availability of content universal.

In the years ahead, online, blended, and distance learning will become positive, personal, and powerful forces in millions of people's lives. In fact, a recent review of research conducted by the United States Department of Education revealed an astonishing finding (Means et al., 2009). When analyzed for effectiveness, blended learning (a combination of online and place-based instruction) was found to be most effective, followed by online learning and classroom instruction, in that order! Even today, traditional instruction is the least effective of the three alternatives.

As you will see in the next two chapters, the new quality criteria for higher education in the future will focus on assessment, personalization, and adaptation, as well as on the customization of the overall learning experience to meet the unique needs of each learner.

8

Game Changers

New Media and the Open Education Resource Movement

As he spoke to the nation after taking the oath of office in January 2009, President Obama addressed the issue of change, and resistance to change. He argued that change was not a choice, but a requirement to adjust to the new realities we face, as a people and as a country. The words he used were simple, but powerful: "The ground has shifted underneath our feet."

In 2008, several months before the election, a respected college president made the following comment to me as we discussed the role of his institution in the context of what they would do with a significant new gift they had recently received.

> When you come to think of it, I could run an entire college without a campus, a course calendar, and all the other things we provide, including a standing faculty the way we use them today. You would want to have subject matter experts and people who knew a great deal about mentoring. And you would want ongoing research and conversation about how adults learn—online and on-ground. But the days when the faculty defined and provided the content, when the college was known for those elements and its research capacity as opposed to its teaching and learning, is over for most colleges. And we sure don't need more of the same. ...

But I'll never do it. The faculty and some of the alumni
would go crazy.

Change comes in many forms, at many times, and in a variety
of places. Some change, like changing an attitude or a behavior,
can be intensely personal. Other change, however, like global
warming or the technology revolution, affects us collectively as
well—personally, socially, civically, and economically.

There are many ways of depicting resistance to change, or
blindness to the implications and ultimate consequences of ignoring change. Imagine a group of dinosaurs, doing what they had
always done, eating grass and whiling away the time in some far
northern reach. It is chillier than normal, but they simply keep on
munching, because they can't comprehend the implications of the
coming cold. Unflinching and without a clue, they ultimately
perish because they didn't head south in front of the changing
climate. The Ice Age was coming, whether they knew it or not.
Today, stubborn resistance to the implications of the technology
revolution will be equally fruitless. This change is unstoppable.

In his illuminating book *Tipping Point*, Malcolm Gladwell
(2000) gave words to the moment in time when the balance shifts
and events cascade in a different direction. His larger point includes
the understanding that, once the tipping point is reached, the
game changes, and the possibilities and requirements for survival
and success change with it. After the tipping point, as with the
bank crisis of 2008–2009, when confidence is gone and credit is
scarce, there is no going back. The only way out is forward, through
the new reality, using new and old tools to address the situation.

We have reached a tipping point in our educational and economic worlds, the point at which the needs for an informed and
appropriately educated citizenry and the capacity to educate them
have tipped away from the status quo, toward an unknown future
that must be invented quickly.

The Law of Thirds describes our current capacity to succeed
with learners. Less than one-third of all ninth graders actually

persist to get some higher education after high school. Our current capacity to educate more people is "maxed out." At the same time, projections for the types and amounts of new jobs being created tell us that our economic and social need for more educated people is growing ever more rapidly. So, our system of education does not have sufficient capacity to produce the success we need. Either we will adapt, change, and succeed educationally or fail socially and economically in the emerging world economic order. The ground has shifted underneath our feet.

Higher education is caught by not only the law of diminishing returns but also some diehard traditions, developed in an earlier time, that do not fit today's rapidly changing world. In his insightful and timely book *Disrupting Class*, Clayton Christiansen (2008) provides a crucial, additional perspective on what needs to happen. The implicit message includes strong reasons why our existing institutions are the wrong places to look for a solution to this new challenge.

Christiansen (2008) draws a distinction between "sustaining" and "disruptive" innovations. A sustaining innovation is a change in degree. It extends existing performance, improving it in the known market. So, a car that goes faster or a plane that flies farther is a sustaining innovation. Having brand new dormitories with Internet cafes and exercise rooms is a sustaining innovation. Institutions do these things to compete, to keep up with their competitors for new students. It is the price of staying in the game, necessary but not always sufficient to provide great educational experiences.

A disruptive innovation, however, is a change in kind. Utterly new, it brings a new product to market that is quite possibly not as useful initially to the known customers as what others have been selling. But, because the product is affordable and easy to use, it addresses a previously untapped market, people whom Christiansen calls "non-consumers." Precisely because the disruptive innovation is new," he writes, "the very definition of what constitutes quality, and therefore what improvement means, is *different* from what quality and improvement mean in the existing market" (2008, p. 47).

Christiansen continues,

> The personal computer is a classic example of a disruptive innovation. Prior to its introduction, the least expensive computer was the minicomputer, the name of which came from the fact that it was much smaller than mainframe computers, which had filled an entire room. But minicomputers cost well over $200 thousand, and required an engineering degree to operate them. The leading minicomputer company was Digital Equipment Company (DEC). During the 1970s and 1980s, DEC was one of the most admired companies in the world economy. But it missed the boat on the PC revolution and was ultimately destroyed by the personal computer. How did this happen?
>
> Apple, one of the pioneers in personal computing, originally sold its model IIe computer as a toy to children. Children had been non-consumers of computers before, so they did not care that the product was not as good as the existing mainframe and minicomputers in solving the problems those computers were designed to solve. None of DEC's customers could even use a personal computer for the first ten years it was on the market because it wasn't good enough for their problems. That meant that the more carefully DEC listened to its best customers, the fewer signals they got that the personal computer mattered—because in fact it didn't— to those customers. (p. 48)

This is a crucial point to consider when the subject is dramatic educational change. Higher education has historically been accredited and regulated within frameworks that actively discourage "disruptive innovation," making it virtually impossible to implement, evaluate, and sustain. So, if we are going to encourage a quantum leap and a change in the way we understand teaching and learning, we must have additional encouragement and permission to do so within the context of external regulation and accreditation, in light of the challenges we face.

Consider the example of exporting curriculum content and the assessment of learning from the classroom to the Web. In this model, responsibility for presenting the material and evaluating learning is no longer the private and individual professional responsibility of each faculty member in a classroom; it is now a responsibility shared between the individual faculty member and instructional designers. They employ a learning outcomes structure with connected rubrics to guide assessment, which is, in turn, evaluated independently by third parties. This model also opens the door for the students' learning to be assessed using the outcomes and the rubrics, even if that learning was not achieved using the "taught" curriculum.

Many faculty members might well describe these types of web-enhanced learning and assessment as less qualitative and valuable than the first. In reality, however, the functions are similar. Curricular content is available. Curricular content is taught. And learning is demonstrated to acceptable standards of achievement. The circumstances, however, are different. The web-enhanced services are geared for a different group of learners, who may well have been, heretofore, nonconsumers. They are offered to deepen the perceived reliability and validity of the learning assessed. The large-scale assessment of learning, separate from teaching, would itself be a disruptive innovation, creating educational opportunity for millions of current nonconsumers.

It is this intersection of innovation and need, converted to opportunity by information technology, that must be protected somehow within the regulatory environment. Otherwise, the traditional view will control the debate, the nonconsumers will have to wait longer for the services they need and deserve, and the nation's workforce will continue to fall short of the needs confronting it.

I had a personal experience that led me from a sustaining to a disruptive innovation during my early days at the Community College of Vermont. We had already made the decision that there would be no campus, that we would take the education to the learners and meet their needs using the existing physical and human resources of the community for classroom space and faculty. We were going to put learning at the center as we took education to the end of the road in rural Vermont.

But we also knew that offering credits and degrees to our target populations would be controversial in the eyes of the traditional institutions in Vermont and some of the political leaders as well. Our students were poor, poorly educated people who, in the view of many in the state's educational and political establishment, didn't deserve credit or degrees. We wanted to dampen the establishment's initial hostility to our program as much as possible in the hopes of easing into a more palatable political environment.

With these concerns in mind, we developed a working concept derived from Ivan Illich's community education "switchboard" model first described in his book, *Deschooling Society* (1971). In this model, we organized the resources for teaching and learning in a public and transparent manner and let the people use the resources as they wished. Everyone was a teacher as well as a learner, and the learning was informal and unrecognized. So, like in Little League baseball or the Girl Scouts, the learning would be largely voluntary and need driven.

One night, I was presenting the concept to a group of child care workers in the rural Northeast Kingdom of Vermont. I had just finished describing this new college, emphasizing that it was designed specifically to bring education to them in places and at times that were convenient. Because it was 1971, the Internet and the World Wide Web were not even a gleam in anyone's eye. Photocopiers were on the cutting edge and gas was 50 cents a gallon. Given this context, we were thinking more in terms of the agricultural extension service and a face-to-face delivery model to deliver our services.

I explained carefully that we would not be tied to academic tradition. There would be, for instance, no campus and no permanent faculty. We would use community resources to support the learning needs of the community. And there would be no credits or degrees, just courses that were valuable to them, like child development.

But one of the women there, Margery, wasn't buying it. There was anger in the air, averted eyes, heavy silence, shifting chairs. "You, with your Princeton degree on the wall, are telling us we don't need one!" Her face flushed and voice rising, Margery continued, "What do you think we are, dumb? We *need* credit. If you're not going to be tied to college traditions, you should start by giving us credit for the things we have already learned working here. If it's good enough for you, Peter, it's good enough for us."

Margery needed help all right, but not the help I was offering. She was trapped by a reality that I had ignored. Everything she knew she had learned raising her family on a Vermont farm and working in the child care center. Although she was very good at her work, colleges and other employers did not recognize or accept that kind of learning when she looked for another job or tried to further her education.

As I drove home that night, I realized that we had to bridge the gap between the personal lives of our students and their college programs, blending the learning they had done informally with courses that would take them further. Thanks to Margery, I understood that some very useful learning may be personal and informal, but that without assessment, credit, and validation it had little value in the larger society. Moreover, without assessment, credit, and validation, Margery's life was devalued as well.

And so, in that moment, I chose the path of disruptive innovation over sustaining innovation. The Community College of Vermont would offer courses and classes, there was no alternative to that. But we would also assess and validate the learning our students had done elsewhere and outside of school, and we would take the steps necessary to offer courses for credit and associate's degrees as an accredited institution. In future years, I came to believe that this decision, fueled by Margery's righteous indignation, actually made the Community College of Vermont's success possible. It gave us a complete and coherent educational identity, something we could stand on, improve, and defend.

When it comes to educational improvement, the paradox we face rests in the space between sustaining and disruptive innovations. Although our current system of higher education has been successful, it needs a series of sustaining innovations that will extend and deepen its reach and its power. Many scholars and associations are working on this challenge. A prime example is the American Association of Colleges and Universities (AACU) and the deeply important work in which they are engaged to strengthen and define liberal education in the twenty-first century.

But if we want to serve the middle third, those adults who have graduated from high school and have had no college experience, we need new designs. Any successful service to these new learners must come in addition to the successes we currently have in place. We need disruptive innovation to meet the new needs that are arising. We must promote and encourage both our traditional successes and new innovations.

Millions of our underserved learners need disruptive innovations that will serve their needs. To build from Christiansen's example (2008), they may not need a mainframe computer (a research university) or a minicomputer (a state university or community college), but they do need

- to have access to information technology,
- to have a learning environment that is friendly to their styles and intelligences,
- to have their learning recognized,
- to have that learning count, and
- to learn more whenever they can.

That, to continue the analogy, may be the equivalent of the personal computer or its emerging derivatives in the world of higher education. America needs disruptive innovation in higher education.

Unfortunately, however, for reasons discussed earlier, our colleges and universities cannot respond effectively and comprehensively to these new challenges. It is extremely difficult if not impossible for them to keep up with the pace of change in the world around them. Here is another possible reason why. They are hard-pressed to test new approaches for effectiveness, given the assumptions and expectations of their faculties and alumni.

Just as it happened to the Digital Equipment Company, paying for and integrating new forms of educational recognition and delivery, and at the same time keeping the traditional customers happy, is nearly impossible. Technology is making things possible that were unimaginable thirty years ago. It looks different and it acts different, presenting a direct challenge to the established campus culture. It is also extremely expensive, posing a significant challenge to tight capital budgets. When the pace of change outside of the academy exceeds the ability for the academy to respond to it, organizationally and financially, the inelasticity of the traditional model is further exposed.

I first encountered the problem of externally driven technological change outpacing the ability to finance renewal of equipment as an educator and a state senator in Vermont. We were looking at how to update and improve a magnificent network of regional vocational centers, which had been built fifteen to twenty years earlier. Their curricula ran the whole gamut of available Vermont occupations at that time, from working with computers to farm machinery operation and repair. And, as regional institutions spread around the state, part of their genius had been that each region could afford something that no one town could support alone. We had maximized resources through cooperation.

Even then, in the early 1980s, it was becoming clear that the same problem, affordability, existed at the regional level as well. We had built the centers, but we had not anticipated the capital costs associated with renewing and continually improving the machinery and technology to keep pace with the change occurring outside of the centers. And change outside the centers was accelerating at rates that outstripped conventional capital reinvestment cycles. So, gradually, like the salt corroding the undercarriage of the car, the curricula became outdated. And, as that happened, it became increasingly difficult for the students to keep up with the reality they would find when they entered the workplace, whether it was the family farm or the IBM plant.

The pace of change outside of the educational institutions was too fast, and the state government didn't have the cash to pay for the continual upgrades that would have met the need. In this case, however, the world outside the vocational centers was also creating a solution to this problem. It turned out that IBM and some of the other major employers in the state had the interest and the resources to think about a different approach. Slowly, a new cooperative model, using two-way video with electronic classrooms, was developed. Through it, over the ensuing decades, workers and students around the state have been able to learn skills and abilities that would otherwise have been unavailable.

Fast forward twenty more years to the World Society of Information Systems (WSIS) global meeting in Tunis. As assistant director general for education at UNESCO, I heard Nicholas Negroponte describe his dream of providing "one laptop for every child." His vision, ambition, and commitment on full display,

Negroponte described the results he had witnessed with children in rural Laos when they were given computers and shown how to operate and maintain them. Even accounting for the exaggeration of the evangelist, the implications for learning in a world in which there were not enough teachers were stunning, and very challenging to a world that assumes all formal learning has to happen in a classroom.

The next project I encountered at WSIS was that of Dr. James Billington, head of the United States Library of Congress. His objective was to harness all the resources of all the major libraries in the world into one global database, bringing the print and related knowledge of the world to the fingertips of all.

As a university president in California, I had some exposure to the power of making educational resources available electronically through two projects. MERLOT (Multi-media Online Resource for Learning and Online Teaching), an early and continuing open education curricular resource for faculty and students, was initially sponsored by the California State University system. MERLOT is a dynamic repository of curricula, complete with evaluations and comments by those who have used it, available to any faculty member or learner who wants to become a member. MERLOT has evolved into an internationally accepted online resource. Its use, however, is largely informal, not integrated with the curricula of universities.

And CalState Teach, an online teacher training program, had gained critical approval for its success. CalState Teach focused on unlicensed elementary school teachers who were working with temporary certificates. The curriculum was built around their daily lesson plans and teaching activities. Organized into cohorts electronically, with each cohort led by an expert, the elementary classroom literally became their learning laboratory for certification.

From its earliest days, CalState Teach has been evaluated as equivalent and usually superior to the more traditional campus-based and intern programs by its students, the supervising teachers, and the school districts sponsoring and hiring the graduates. Because it is Web based and learner centered, however, the program has not grown in scope since early in its history, stifled by opposition from faculty who work in the traditional teacher-training programs.

More recently, as a member of the MIT/OpenCourseWare Advisory Board, I had a front-row seat at one of the most disruptive innovations in American higher education: providing thousands of courses free for anyone who wanted to view them. Beyond the public library, Ben Franklin's "Poor Man's University," this innovation actually organizes the knowledge and lets the learner "graze" through it, without restrictions. It is sort of like an intellectual buffet.

But there, in Tunis, with Negroponte's and Billington's efforts added to the mix, I saw the true implications of the emerging Open Education Resource (OER) movement. Advocated by such leaders as the Hewlett Foundation and UNESCO, the OER movement will make all manner of curricular resources, including full courses, available ultimately to anyone, anywhere, for little or no money. It will promote collaboration and participation driven by the consumer as well as by institutions in which exclusion and individual activity had previously been the rule. It gives personal learners vast new resources to support their learning projects. People pursuing the learning projects first identified by Allen Tough have just found a new resource. And personal learning just got its campus: the World Wide Web populated by the OER movement and myriad other information resources.

Availability of organized information in an OER format is, however, only the opening scene in what is rapidly becoming an epic novel. The OER movement, by making this material available, will indirectly drive a new and enhanced focus on new forms of learning and organizing education. These forms will include the assessment of learning, personalized services, and academic planning as separate but essential parts of the educational experience.

As we discussed in "Learning Is More Than Strictly Academic," there are constraints in the traditional model when this new world of opportunity presents itself. For example, the traditional evaluation of learning, "how you did" in the course, usually boils down to the common practices of the dominant model: showing up to class regularly and performing on tests or in papers. But understanding what you know is a different, more complex matter than "how you did."

Good assessment, and the reflection that comes with it, generates the moment when learning occurs, when meaning is extracted from experience. As millions of personal learners use these courses and other learning resources, long unavailable to them, the demand for flexible, low-cost assessment of that learning that measures "knowing" as well as performance will escalate. These current nonconsumers are another huge new market.

Improving undergraduate teaching and learning has been a priority for years. Up to this point, however, a college's reputation has been based largely on the quality of its historical status, research, faculty, curriculum, and selectivity, not its teaching and learning. Very few institutions have risen to the top because they were judged to be excellent at teaching and learning or adding value for a student. In fact, academic leaders are pretty clear about the fact that research, even research critical to the disciplines, science, and the national interest, has little to do with the quality of undergraduate teaching and learning.

Another constraint is filled with irony. The further you proceed in education, the more proficient you become and the more you know, the more expensive you become to the institution. We routinely pack freshmen—those who need the most learning support, mentoring, and attention—into large lecture halls. And we reserve the small seminars and individual attention from professors for seniors and graduate students. All of this has persisted as yet another "dangerous conceit." Why? Because content in the curriculum, and the quality of research and scholarship, rather than contact with the learner, are seen as the primary distinguishing characteristics of quality in higher education.

The ever-weakening relationship between perceived curricular quality and senior research faculty members at established universities has, however, been even further eroded by the OER movement. This floodtide of high-quality course materials into the open resource space has permanently established a new balance between content, the learner, and recognized learning. It marks the end of curricular content as a distinguishing feature for most of higher education.

The developments at Apple's iTunes U, the Global OpenCourseWare Consortium, Facebook, and Wikiversity are further evidence of this movement. All of these resources will continue to reshape the perceived value characteristics of higher education toward personalization, adaptation, and higher quality.

Although we are in the early stages of this education era, Web 2.0 and information technology already offer higher education several profound advantages that have been heretofore unattainable. These advantages are improvements on the parallel practices that are currently predominant on most campuses. As a core delivery and support system for learning services of all kinds, information technology brings at least three additional advantages: flexibility, consistency, and diversity. These built-in capacities can make Web-based and blended academic services better than those at place-based, traditional programs, giving them a distinct qualitative advantage.

Flexibility

The primary argument in favor of technology-assisted distance learning over the years has been access. Whether it was the old television show *Sunrise Semester* or video-linked lectures that were shown in community learning centers or on islands off the coast of Maine, the idea was to bring the education to the person who needed education.

Evaluation showed that programs like these worked relatively well at expanding access, as long as they were perceived by the learner to be the best educational alternative available at the time. This makes sense. People would settle for a delivery model for education if their need was great enough and it was the best one available.

At the same time, however, access without flexibility in the curriculum and other learning support strategies had severe constraints. Being able to listen to a lecture over the television and phone in your questions to the faculty member was novel, well intentioned, and better than nothing. But it was not that effective. And in those "horse and buggy days" of community-based postsecondary education, everyone, those who offered the programs and those who consumed them, knew they were settling for a compromised model. Nevertheless, it was truly the best we could do at the time.

Today, the balance has changed. Flexibility is the emerging norm. Learning is now possible anytime and anywhere you can get a signal or plug in your device. Sophisticated content and support services can be offered in interactive formats that are more closely customized to the needs of the learner. And, even as campuses struggle to afford and employ increasingly sophisticated technology and teaching and learning strategies to better serve their customers, the world beyond the campuses is speeding ahead ever more quickly.

Campuses are caught in a hostile capital reinvestment cycle with resulting limitations on their capital and physical models. They can neither control nor sustain investment at rates that satisfy the need and match the capacity and potential beyond their doors. To compound this growing gap, the "social environment," the space in which Americans currently operate technologically, is becoming more sophisticated and customized every day. Learners today have more potential and greater capacity to access and use information than many institutions have to offer it.

Web 2.0 and emerging information technology devices and services make the delivery of high-quality, personalized learning possible anywhere, anytime for the current nonconsumers of campus-based higher education. They also make the assessment of learning gained in other ways and settings available for these new learners, bringing the value of their professional and life experiences directly into the degree structure and learning recognition process on a previously unimaginable scale.

What we used to think of as "flexibility" assumed a core of content and a variation on the traditional delivery model. What we have today is actually an entirely new design proposition for education, one on which I will elaborate in Chapter Nine. We have the tools to rethink how we organize and present the services we offer.

Now, formally recognized learning does not have to be bounded by a static curriculum, a physical location, or a faculty knowledge base and schedule. Learning can be enhanced by design to include gaming and other simulation technology, adaptive assessments that respond to learning styles and remediate immediately, Web-based peer support, and a myriad of other previously unimaginable resources. By organizing these new resources for learning, all who deserve access can achieve it. As such, access will become obsolete as an educational goal. The new goal, the challenge for tomorrow, is education success for the middle third of adult learners, who are currently beyond the margin of higher education.

Consistency

Using a Web-based curriculum, it is possible to achieve a heretofore impossible level of consistency in exposure to materials and ideas as well as in the assessment of learning within any course or across any program.

On a traditional campus, if one hundred faculty members teach the same curriculum in one hundred classrooms, there is no way to determine that the students in those classrooms have received equivalent experiences. We don't know what content was actually taught. Nor do we know what evaluation standards were used. We don't even know, for sure, that a given course links effectively with the preceding course or the one that will follow, let alone with broader program and degree objectives.

In fact, as the faculty at California State University, Monterey Bay, discovered in a courageous and thoughtful study they performed, without constant attention to the details there is little alignment among or between the course objectives actually taught and received. At the individual class-session level, there was little alignment between what the faculty members thought they were teaching and what the students thought they were being taught. Discovering this disconnect drove the faculty to further alignment of teaching and objectives, within and among courses.

This type of quality assurance would be a far different matter, however, if those one hundred faculty members were using the same Web-based curriculum as a foundation for their teaching in a blended, asynchronous format. Although protecting the right of each faculty member to teach as he or she deems most successful—using teams, individual study, or other techniques—the different media and materials provided would be consistent, giving significant horizontal stability at the same time. And uniform learning outcomes and rubrics supporting them in each course would add tremendous consistency and reliability to the assessment of the learning students achieved.

No one would argue that exposure to the same materials and assessments would equal the same level of learning among students. But this approach does create the basis for far better quality assessment of teaching and learning, which can then be linked to continuous improvement of both.

Consider the following general education program concept as a case in point. It integrates the basic general education disciplines throughout the curriculum so students learn how these disciplines apply to their prospective professions. The program also promotes collaboration between disciplines and makes general education the responsibility of the entire university.

Students are required to take six courses that introduce them to the fundamental concepts of the five basic ways of knowing: communication, mathematics, science, social science, and arts and humanities. These interdisciplinary courses help students understand how these fields apply to their personal and professional lives.

In addition to these courses, however, every other course at the university includes a unit of study from one of these five fields or from three other topics: ethics, critical thinking, and research. These units of study, embedded in each course and supported by learning outcomes and rubrics, show the student how this content applies to the course. The net effect of this model is that all students are continually exposed to general education content throughout their program of studies.

For example, an ethics unit in a criminal justice course might present ethical dilemmas faced by police officers and how to handle them. An arts and humanities unit embedded in a nursing course might show how creating visual art improves the healing process. Finally, each course includes a writing assignment that is graded by the professor, using a university standard rubric, and all professors are professionally trained in how to use the rubric to evaluate student writing (Sanders, 2008).

Without an outcomes-based curriculum, supported by carefully developed rubrics and delivered consistently in an online format, the quality and consistency that are the hallmarks of this program would be impossible to achieve.

The same consistency can be built into the learning outcomes for any course or program. This is a significant advantage for every learner and every teacher. For the learners, it gives them unparalleled ability to focus on the outcomes they are trying to achieve in the curriculum. This is a great benefit to learners who benefit from knowing what they are expected to learn and having examples of just what that learning might look like. No longer is successful completion of a course a guessing game, intellectual Russian roulette in which the winners proceed and the losers go home.

For the teaching faculty, this learning environment is rich in opportunities to work their craft within a clear pedagogical framework. In it, they are able to achieve consistency across the curriculum while focusing like lasers on the chosen results of the curriculum. Every learning outcome in a course and a program can be supported with consistent rubrics to assure a high degree of reliability in the learning students achieve.

This consistency, in turn, creates a far more stable and accurate basis for determining quality while describing different levels of learning attainment and academic success across the population of learners, teachers, and courses. In a world in which people are interested in what you know and are able to do as a result of your academic program, information technology brings a second great asset to learning: consistency connected to results.

Finally, this new era in media allows us to look past the time-based curriculum, in which learners must produce results within a given period. Insisting on a time-based curriculum, a necessary feature in the pretechnology era, has become yet another "dangerous conceit," limiting successful learning in traditional colleges. The new goal can be mastery of learning within an extended or shortened time frame.

Diversity

Personalization and quality learning are among the new distinguishing features of the "new designs" for higher education. The keys to achieving them lie in our emerging technology and new media. In a Web-based or blended, learner-centered university, we can achieve and maintain curricular consistency at levels that were previously unattainable. At the same time, however, we can dramatically increase the personalization of services to each learner, molding the learning experience to the needs of each. There will be a remarkable diversity of services through personalization and adaptation.

We can use exercises to generate diagnostic information about how each learner learns best. We can adapt the material and the learning requirements to serve each student's learning profile and focus on the areas where each student is weak. And we can personalize the advice, counseling, and degree-planning efforts so that each learner has a personal learning plan that supports his or her degree work and life aspirations.

Even as consistency is added to the course content and outcomes, game-changing technology and software open a new arena for great teaching. The technology takes care of all the things that machines and processes can do—presenting material through simulations, through direct links, or in other ways. At the same time, students know the standards for the course in question because they are public information. The learners can look at the rubrics and understand the different levels of accomplishment that will get them a superior or merely a passing grade. Rubrics are connected to a hierarchy of knowledge use, such as that outlined in Bloom's taxonomy (Bloom & Krathwohl, 1956). They can return to this information as many times as they like, studying it and using it to learn.

This frees the faculty member to do what only people can do—listen, counsel, advise, teach, clear up confusions, and evaluate the learning that has occurred.

Information technology makes a vast galaxy of diverse learning resources available to enrich curricula. No longer are the faculty members, or the learners, constrained by resources known to them, such as the local library. Now, as any curriculum is being built, the vast resources of the Internet are available to enrich the mix. And, as they absorb any curriculum, the learners have an almost unlimited variety of accessible, high-quality resources to augment their learning. This is a far cry from the "supplemental reading lists" of my generation and a deeply enriching element for moving learning forward. As Kevin Carey put it in "What Colleges Should Learn from Newspapers' Decline,"

> As of today, there is no Craigslist destroying the financial foundations of the modern university. Teaching is a lot more complicated than advertising, and universities have the advantage of sitting behind government-backed barriers to competition, in the form of accreditation. Anyone can use the Internet to sell classified ads or publish opinion columns or analyze the local news. Not anyone can sell credit-bearing courses or widely recognized degrees.
>
> But the number of organizations that can—and are doing it online—is getting bigger every year.
>
> And it would be a grave mistake to assume that the regulatory walls of accreditation will protect traditional universities forever. Elite institutions like Stanford University and Yale University are giving away extremely good lectures on the Internet, free. Web sites like Academic Earth are organizing those and thousands more like them into "playlists," which is really just iPod-speak for "curricula." Every year the high schools graduate another three million students who have never known a world that worked any other way. (2009)

Taken collectively, these "Game Changers" are radically revising the relationships between universities and the communities and people around them. Built for an information-scarce society, colleges traditionally offered the special service of access to faculty and programs not attainable elsewhere. Caught in a rising tide of information and technology, these same institutions' once-special services and standing are now outflanked by developments in the world around them.

As we will see in Chapter Nine, this information-rich world is spawning the raw material from which new types of programs and services will be invented. These institutions, Colleges for the Twenty-First Century, will be creatures of this emerging world as surely as the current structure of the university is a creature of the information-scarce society of the past.

As we create new designs for higher education, our thinking must be "disruptive" to the status quo, though it must also fit the dynamics of the situation that lies ahead. New types of colleges will allow us to bring the next third of our population—people with high school diplomas who have not been able to get to and persist in college—into the sunshine of educational success. We will tap their unrecognized talents, bringing benefits to them and to the larger society.

9

Reaching the Middle Third

Talent-Friendly Colleges for the Twenty-First Century (C21Cs)

American public policy has been committed to equal opportunity and educational access for all since the passage of the major education legislation and the Civil Rights Act in the 1960s. Building on the GI Bill, the country opened its arms to the Jeffersonian belief that merit and equal opportunity matter more than birth, wealth, race, or gender.

As we approach the second decade of the twenty-first century, we can move beyond using the concept of merit to screen out those who do not qualify. We can now treat the creation of merit as an active and positive concept, screening in people who otherwise might not have been given the opportunity to succeed. A new goal is within our reach: to create, sustain, and enhance merit through education.

For the first time in history, we have the knowledge and the tools available to educate through new designs. This capacity is driven by the stark economic and social need to make college-level success a reality for many more people. The title of this chapter refers to Colleges for the Twenty-First Century, or C21Cs. I have coined this term as shorthand to label the new approaches and models that can be created and implemented as we take the steps necessary to double our educational output.

Emerging information technology and Web 2.0 have permanently changed the possibilities and potential of higher education.

With the decline of content as the critical determinant of quality, there are three overarching quality indicators that support "merit for the many": personalization, customization, and mobility.

Personalization happens when we connect the entire process of education to the life of the learner. Allen Tough's research has documented that learning happens naturally and continuously, occurring when there is a strong connection between the "it" of whatever is to be learned and the "me" of the lived experience of the learner. That is why the adult's learning projects are so seamless within the learner's life.

The more personally connected the learner is to his or her learning program, the higher the likelihood of success. The less that a formal learning program engages each learner's experience, interests, aspirations, and culture, the less likely it is that the necessary human connections will be made. Almost one hundred years ago, John Dewey, the great education philosopher, made the same point in *Democracy and Education* (1916). He imagined a synergy between the experience of living and more formal, organized education. And he thought that schools built and used for that purpose could successfully incorporate the lived experience of every learner.

When it comes to personalization, yesterday's philosophy is today's practical reality.

Customization is the process through which the learning experience is adapted to the needs of the learner without lowering standards. Former U.S. Secretary of Labor and senator Bill Brock (2001) compared learning to seeing, saying that it is a natural or instinctive activity. He notes that most testing is intended to determine a student's progress, when, in fact, we should be measuring a learner's ability to learn and identifying the learning style that best fits him or her. Brock says that when a learner is struggling, instead of seeing how we are failing the learner, we

> buy new educational resources, fix the curriculum, we
> invest in new labs and learning centers, we buy new

computers, we do everything we can to adjust the externals we control. And when all else fails, we beat up on faculty and we beat up on learners.

As parents, we never, never would treat our sick son or daughter the way we treat learners who struggle in school. If you and I had a child with a 103-degree temperature, a bad stomach ache, cold sweats, and tremors, we never would think of suggesting, "Come on Bill, you're not trying hard enough to get well." We would take him to the doctor, find out what was going on, and have it fixed. (Brock, 2001)

Customization in higher education will have many elements, including amassing diagnostic information for each learner. Good diagnostic information will help all involved—faculty, learners, parents—better understand the individual learning profile of each learner, describing how each person learns best. Just as good medical information allows doctors to adapt treatment to the patient's condition and related pathology, good educational information will allow educators and learners to adapt learners' individual programs to their needs. The day has come when good diagnostic assessment can be seamlessly integrated into the curriculum and the pedagogy, aiding teacher and learner alike.

Mobility is the capacity to take the learning you have achieved and have it "count" for employment or further education wherever you go. C21Cs will acknowledge the reality of mobility, treating transfer credit and learning done elsewhere more equally. As I will discuss later in this chapter, treating academic credit like colonial currencies based on the source is an enormous obstacle to mobility. It is also, in an age when thorough assessments of each learner and their learning are possible, as unnecessary as it is destructive.

Some people will view these assertions with irony and skepticism. How can it possibly be, they will ask, that personalization, customization, and mobility can be dominant characteristics in a media environment that serves millions of people simultaneously? Is it simply a rhetorical device, a word trick? Or can we achieve personal, customized treatment in this environment and at the scale needed?

To them, I would say, learning and education are personal to each learner. Education, and the learning that drives it, are based on relationships. At the heart of it, there is only one person for whom learning, education, and life happens up close and personal, and that is the learner. Each of us is, as a personal learner, the conductor of a personal symphony, an artist with a private canvas. That said, in the eyes of that learner, educational services that anticipate learner needs and respond to them are personalized and customized. The great gift that emerging technological capacity gives us is to personalize learning to each person's interests, strengths, and needs.

As such, personalization and customization have as many faces as there are learners. Our emerging technological capacity and the end of scarcity dramatically enhance our ability to achieve both with every learner. Now, in these new paradigms, learners can get recognition for their personal learning and participate in high-quality, Web-based education programs with curricula tailored to their specific needs.

In the talent-friendly College for the Twenty-First Century, services will be organized around the needs of the learner, not the habits of the institution. Sharing common characteristics, C21Cs will tap into a new ecology of learning that supports personalized and customized learning around the world. And their purposes will include creating and then validating merit in each learner.

Beyond simply admitting students and moving them toward the degrees or certificates they choose, the C21C will be organized to support a lifetime "learning support" partnership with all its students. The talent-friendly C21C will comprise at least five elements, some operating within the college, some operating on the outside. The potential to implement them in a comprehensive and integrated fashion exists today. For maximum effect, they should be implemented in an integrated way, serving as the DNA of a new institutional format for supporting learning in the twenty-first century.

Some of these elements are "developmental" and not in widespread play today. Others, however, are already known and used in some institutions. Taken collectively in the context of a new ecology of learning, they suggest a new universe of possibilities for higher education that moves beyond place-based degree attainment and positions the college as the preferred, lifelong higher education partner for individual learners as well as business and nonprofit organizations.

The list of examples offered here are only a suggestion of what lies ahead. Other examples of C21C practices and applications, and additional characteristics of this new ecology of learning will be created by people as they occupy the space and experiment with alternatives. These elements are intended as a starting point to an extended developmental discussion.

End-to-End Service: Superb Support Throughout the Relationship

The concept of learner support will expand to encompass the entire student experience from the first touch in admissions to the last learning project the student undertakes in partnership with the college. Operating as part of a lifelong partnership between college and learner, student support will still include the wide variety of services that we associate with learning support today, including remediation, tutoring, career exploration, and all forms of academic counseling. The whole service, however, will dive deeper and swim farther than we have considered to date.

At the C21C's core will be an educational portfolio. It will operate as a collection point for all of the learner's information as well as a "point of service" for connecting learning to work and meeting other needs that the learner might have. The "look and feel" of the portfolio will match the technological environment the learner is experiencing socially, creating social space in which learning and related activities can happen easily and informally (Ittelson, 2008).

The C21C will, of course, retain the authority to make critical determinations about the quality and amount of learning. And it will offer mentoring and advice. Its basic attitude, however, will be less hierarchical and more of that of partner or lifelong associate to the learner, providing seamless support, including diagnostics, education planning, and career management and advice.

End-to-end service will begin with a unique "on-boarding" process for all learners. Starting with a free offer of information and diagnostic services in a flexible, open-resource social space, it would also include standardized diagnostic tests that are administered to the vast majority of new students during their first term of study. The tests will diagnose the skills, interests, and values of each learner as well as their motivation, providing critical information to the students as well as the college.

Armed with this information, the learner becomes a better consumer of the college's services, and the college can adapt to the needs of the learner more fluidly. The on-boarding process will close with a reflective assignment, sometimes called a "success plan," in which the learners individually lay out what they have learned and how they will move forward (www.open.ac.uk, 2009).

Because this will be the beginning, ideally, of a lifelong partnership between the learner and the institution, every student will also develop a lifelong learning portfolio. Among other things, the portfolios will provide a vehicle for laying out students' programs of study, showing where their transfer credits fit, and determining which courses will fill out their degree and career plans. The portfolio will create and incorporate the capability to list each outcome students must master to earn their degrees and be successful in their chosen careers.

As students complete their courses and demonstrate mastery of outcomes, these can be checked off and documented with student work products, test scores, and other evaluation evidence. This becomes a record of student achievement that the students can use in a variety of ways. Ultimately, these outcomes will also be directly articulated to agreed-upon workplace skill sets, connecting each learner's experience and knowledge directly with employer expectations and job skill requirements.

The C21C student support model will rely on dedicated student advisors, who provide student support throughout the college experience. Advisors will be proactive in their support, available whenever the student has a question or need. They will make use of diagnostic information as they work with students. This information will produce a profile for each student that gives the university the ability to understand how different types of students perform in its courses. Over time, research based on this information will give the university the ability to predict performance; give better advice to its students; and improve courses by adapting the learning experiences to the needs of the learners, building in options that accommodate different approaches to learning.

Assessing how students learn best and diagnosing such attributes as study skills and career interests shifts the focus from what the institution does to what the learners need. It makes learners and learning the center of the higher education universe. This is different from the instructional model in most institutions. In most colleges and universities, individual professors decide what content will be taught and how students will be assessed on that content. Then, it is delivered in a "take it or leave it" fashion. If students fail to master the knowledge, it is their fault, not the fault of the faculty member or the institution.

The College for the Twenty-First Century makes a different statement. It says that although the standards for student learning will not be modified, learners will be given important information and advice on what and how to learn, aimed at maximizing their performance. The long-term goal is to provide a variety of learning materials and activities in courses in order to adapt the instruction to the student and so that the student will eventually master the knowledge.

Outcomes-Based Assessment and Consistent Course Design

In a world in which information, knowledge, and job specifications are changing ever more rapidly, outcomes evaluations at the course and program levels are the only consistent means for understanding the relationship between what someone has done and what he or she knows as a result of doing it. Increasingly, employers are asking for skills and abilities at two levels. First, they want employees to be able to write well, think critically and analytically, solve problems, work on a team, and have a global perspective. Second, they would like employees to have demonstrable knowledge in the skill and professional areas required for proficiency in their fields (Jones, 2009).

Managing the interface of the learners and their learning with the changing requirements of the outside world is another aspect of the student support services offered by the C21C. In this model, the college will maintain a continuously updated transcript, connecting the collegiate learning not only to a degree-certificate structure but also to known workplace requirements. This transcript, part of the learner's portfolio, will have a value beyond its total of credits and degrees because it represents consistency, validity, and accuracy. In a highly mobile world, having an ePortfolio that travels with you and is based on valid, reliable, and consistently evaluated learning outcomes will be a significant advantage for the learner as worker and the employer as well.

Curriculum and course development at the C21C will be a team effort, with a consistent course template as the basis for design. It might look like this: faculty members with specific content expertise work with assistant deans of curriculum to design the courses. Following the process referred to as "backward design," outcomes are then vetted by an advisory board (Wiggins & McTighe, 2005). After assessments for each outcome have been created, the course developer then selects learning resources, such as textbooks, journal articles, and Web sites. Next, he or she creates learning activities with these resources and sequences them for optimal student learning. At this point, the course is handed off to a team of instructional designers, who create the learning activities that require such media as video, flash animation, or graphics. They also format the course according to university standards for visuals, titles, and icons, before loading the finished course on the learning management system.

This standardized course development process results in reliable, clear standards on which students can focus, while enabling a robust quality assurance system. It ensures that students enrolled in different sections of the same course have a consistent experience. And, for students who want to study more independently and in a non-time-based environment, the outcomes will be available outside as well as within the course structure.

Professors can employ different teaching styles and methods, but the students are pursuing the same outcomes, using the same materials, and engaging in the same activities. The consistent curriculum also enables quality assurance by supporting curriculum evaluation. University researchers can track student satisfaction and performance in the courses over time and across formats, such as online versus on-campus delivery.

Many institutions that serve adult learners at a distance use a centralized course development process. However, the vast majority of U.S. universities leave course development as well as implementation to the discretion of individual professors. With different designs, outcomes, texts, and learning activities, there is little consistency or quality assurance. This process of course development and presentation also results in inconsistent student experiences and varied quality of instruction. This inconsistency means there is no consistent way to assess the quality of the courses or of the learning itself. Assessment of student achievement in these institutions is reduced to general measures of student ability or portfolios of student work, which indicate that students have met broad program outcomes. C21Cs will be both more precise and more consistent in their learning assessments.

Traditionally, credit has been awarded based on time in class, or seat time. Although the student has to undertake whatever assignments the professor requires in the class, the whole calculus for credit is based on seat time. Moving to outcomes to determine credit improves consistency and quality in teaching as well as learning assessment. Supported by the course and outcome design and the technology, the main points of content and the outcomes required for successful completion are constants in the design. It also, however, allows for teaching and learning flexibility by giving faculty members the latitude to teach the material in the ways they think are most effective.

Finally, learning outcomes give learners clear information on what they will be required to do in a course in order to succeed. You can't learn to ride a bicycle by reading a book. Similarly, if the expectations in a learning experience are not clearly described, learners will have a far more difficult time mastering the content. The talent-friendly College of the Twenty-First Century will use outcomes assessment to determine credit, because it focuses on learning assessment, not teaching and seat time.

There are several colleges and universities that have focused heavily on this type of assessment. Alverno College and Thomas Edison State College have implemented and consistently improved a comprehensive outcomes assessment process for their students for many years. And, more recently, the Western Governor's University and Kaplan University have organized their learning and quality initiatives around specifying course outcomes, assessing them directly.

In a highly mobile society, in which individuals experience multiple job changes during their lifetimes, having transcripted learning that is consistently evaluated, reliable, and accurate is extremely valuable to learners and employers alike. Clear standards and reliable assessments will become key quality indicators in the twenty-first century.

Flexible, Accredited Programs of Study and Degree Plans

Education has its own Long Tail—the growth of easily accessible content, other educational services, and related information on the Web. Course content, whether posted by individuals, companies, traditional colleges and universities, or other nonprofits, is becoming ever more abundant and available. Along with the content, there will also be innumerable free and low-cost services to help informal learners go about their business in a high-support, social atmosphere.

The C21C must be organized to provide services and value to the learners that they can't get someplace else. This suggests that content, although necessary to stimulate learning, will no longer be the critical distinguishing feature. Ultimately, what the learner knows and is able to do as a result of his or her learning will become the critical characteristic. And the means, practices, and strategies that produce high levels of learning recognition and attainment will contribute the value. They will be the hallmarks of quality.

As part of this shift, the architecture and focus of programs of study will assume more importance. Degree and program structures will no longer be the sole artifacts of the faculty and the discipline, largely fixed and inflexible, with requirements and prerequisites added according to faculty members' instincts. The organizing architecture for certificates and degrees will be more flexible and better able to organize and accommodate learning that is highly specific to the needs and interests of the learner and the employer, while also continuing to support learning that is highly structured because of its regulatory or professional considerations.

Organization of learning within the new architecture will also evolve to include new symbols for the learning students accomplish. It will support the concept of a continuing journey that acknowledges learning throughout life, not simply a predetermined destination defined by a degree level. These recognitions of learning will include, but not be limited to, the use of credits and the current degrees.

There will also be new levels of learning recognition. Some will further populate the space within degrees, using "stacked" certificates and other recognitions that document each stage of the learning journey. Others will recognize learning that lies outside of conventional curricula. For example, Six Sigma, a management consulting methodology, has been successful with the awarding of "belts" to its practitioners for demonstrating certain levels of expertise. And Cisco, the high tech company, has been successful in branding their certificates as sufficiently qualitative to warrant employer and collegiate recognition.

The American College of Testing (ACT, www.americancollegeoftesting.org), moreover, has recently developed an emerging type of competency organization and recognition. ACT has developed a national certificate for workplace competencies based on extensive interviews with employers and precise profiling of job skills in each existing job category. They have then organized four levels of performance, ranging from bronze to platinum, by which student performance can be evaluated. It would be a powerful improvement to create a two-way articulation agreement to "map" these competencies—reflecting the worker's knowledge, skills, and abilities—to outcomes-based degree and certificate programs at colleges and universities, thus giving the worker advanced standing at the college for learning done at work. Such an arrangement would also give students at the college a recognized prequalification for workforce placement.

There will only be more of these examples in the future. I can well imagine other hierarchies of learning that operate within a specialty area or simply recognize the accumulation of knowledge and expertise in an area of endeavor. Using agreements, credit equivalencies, and other forms of recognition in a comprehensive approach, all this learning will be available for the learner's portfolio and for formal academic recognition.

The C21C will offer learners, through its lifelong partnership with them, the opportunity to continually rethink and reshape their learning plans and objectives as their needs change. And the recognition structure will reshape and change as well.

In this development, undergraduate degree plans will assume a more learner-oriented focus. It is a common occurrence for degree programs to become cluttered with prerequisites and other requirements that severely limit the learners' ability to adapt the actual studying and learning to their needs within a larger set of requirements. In far too many cases, the things that a student "must" study prevail over the things that a student wants and needs to study. This is yet another conceit, and one in which faculty teaching preferences and academic tradition trump student learning needs, workplace and workforce priorities, and social and civic needs.

This new architecture will anticipate learning outcomes that respond to general education purposes, major requirements, and elective courses. It will also, however, provide flexibility for students, leaving significant space for interpretation and thus encouraging a greater role for personal degree planning and design. Also important, the universal degree plan will also award transfer credit to students who have attended other universities, so they don't lose credit. In addition to transfer credit, the plan will also support experiential credit, credit by examination, and credit earned in corporate classrooms or in the military.

Beyond the generic degree plan, the C21C will also accommodate students by offering interdisciplinary degrees in such areas as Liberal Studies and Professional Studies, as a core part of the learning support and recognition architecture. These degrees enable students to design degree plans that not only draw on their previous experiences and education but also address their educational goals. Students will be able to design "majors" that are personalized to their past and future needs by combining courses from various schools and colleges within or outside the C21C as well as from the Long Tail of content and their own experiential learning.

Facilitating Seamless Transitions Between Life, Work, and Degree Programs

In a century that will be characterized, among other things, by mobility, social choice, flexibility, and speed, the population of learners will be mobile as well. In this environment, mobility for the learning that has been achieved will lie at the heart of the learners' expressed needs. Learning accomplished at work, whether experiential or applied, will translate to the college degree plan seamlessly and be counted toward graduation without losing its value. And learning done in life, in the military, through testing, or at other colleges will translate similarly to credits of equivalent value in the workplace.

We need to create the ability to move and apply learning seamlessly to address the demand that mobility creates. There are two keys to this seamless transition. First, there must be agreement around excellent, outcomes-based assessments that reflect agreed-upon standards of capacity and performance. Second, the learning students have done will be continuously recorded and honored in their portfolios by their learning partner, the C21C. Learners may learn and assess simultaneously. They may learn and then assess later on. Or they may find independent ways to verify their learning, which are then communicated to the C21C.

Learners will take their learning with them throughout life, carrying it in continuously evolving portfolios. Based on learning outcomes, learners' portfolios will be accepted at other institutions and understood by employers, functioning as a new resume with a common language, linking education, life learning, and work. In this scenario, learners should be able to make their own decisions, comparing the services and talent-friendliness of different institutions and avoiding unwitting entrapment in unfriendly institutional policies.

But, if all this is going to work, one critical component is missing. There has to be a *universal common denominator for academic credit*. When traveling on the interstate highway system, you can get on and off wherever you like, as many times as you want, while you travel. Other than time, speed limits, the occasional toll booth, and the need for gas, there are no external constraints. You can drive any registered vehicle and program your own itinerary.

Not so with academic credit in higher education. Academic credit is more like the currencies of the various states during the period of time when our country was governed by the Articles of Confederation. Each state had its own currency, sometimes multiple currencies, and none of it matched another. If enough commerce developed, two states might develop a bartering system that allowed them to exchange and value each other's currency. The debate about a national bank and national currency continued, in one form or another, for almost one hundred years.

But higher education has added an additional, subtle complexity. We not only have multiple currencies but also reserve the right to value each of them, based on how we feel about the sending institution. So, we have multiple currencies and additional multiple valuations of each currency. How can we move from these multiple valuations to an interstate highway system, charted by an Academic GPS (Guidance, Planning, Success)? This element of seamlessness is the last remaining barrier to the adult-friendly college of the twenty-first century.

We must overcome two obstacles: one mathematical and the other behavioral. In this case, the math is easy. By quantifying learning using outcomes, it is a simple enough matter to aggregate "credit" value based on credit equivalencies. Measuring outcomes and equivalencies based on outcomes gives a true recounting of what you know and can do. In other words, learners, as they move through life, from institution to institution, would be able to equate their learning through a "common denominator," creating credit equivalencies that institutions and employers alike would respect.

It will be far more difficult, however, to change institutional behavior. As discussed in "Learning Is More Than Strictly Academic" and "You Can't Get There from Here," there are a wide variety of reasons given to deny credit for experiential learning and "discount" learning done anywhere other than the home institution. As a result, military learning; life experience; and other collegiate, corporate, and proficiency-tested learning are all heavily if not completely discounted by the receiving institution in too many cases.

The talent-friendly C21C will be committed to the recognition of learning, wherever and however it is gained, and its portability. Learners will know the expectations of the college and the consequences of those expectations for their learning.

Learning recognition and portability (LRP) is the next generation of learning assessment, created not for the institution but for the learner. Employing a suite of self-paced and course-based services, LRP, a free-standing service, will assess all learning through equivalencies, validate it, record it, value it in a degree plan, and give the learner the tools to search out his or her best higher education fit. Criteria for the "fit" will include the time required to obtain a degree, cost, and convenience as well as other criteria more personal to the learner. Coupled with the course-level assessment, an outcomes-based architecture, and flexible transfer policies similar to those developed in Europe through the Bologna Process, these degree policies bring an era of global credit portability to our doorsteps.

Others may try to bring order to the expensive chaos that currently dogs learners' transitions from college to work and back through political, legal, and regulatory action. Although some of that may be necessary, I propose another approach: creating a service like LendingTree.com, with which students can evaluate their choices and choose the one best for them. LendingTree lets you assess banks before taking a loan, and Progressive Insurance advertises the value of having you evaluate other insurance companies before buying insurance. It is time to let the students do their own shopping and comparisons, creating a competitive environment for the institutions that want to serve them.

LRP will give students full recognition of their learning and let them move their transcripts among any set of institutions they wish, seeking the best fit. The services will be externally and internally quality assured, and a national consortium of institutions will pledge to use consistent equivalency measures for placing students.

But the C21C will do more than simply subscribe to the Academic GPS. It will also offer flexible, outcomes-based courses and degrees and join the LRP consortium, because it believes that adults should get recognition for all the applicable learning they have done. The new dimension in higher education that I envision will include one or more consortia of institutions that publicly guarantee transfer rates and equivalencies to assist incoming students' decision making. This makes both programmatic and educational sense for each college in the consortium. They will fill their classes, but they will also help learners increase their opportunities, while offering society a more dynamic population as a resource.

Portability of Credit Using the Academic GPS

As we learned in Chapter Eight, "Game Changers," the role of information technology and Web 2.0 is essential to the success of the C21C. It is one thing for people to become increasingly mobile, to be able to learn anything, anytime, anyplace. It is quite another thing, however, to create binding and transparent agreements for the transfer of credit for learning. If, however, even with those other revolutionary changes, learners' recognized learning is not simply and effortlessly portable, they will be penalized both in the "learnplace" by additional time and cost to gain the degree and in the workplace by the inability to move up the ladder of promotion.

With mobility increasing, the demands for credit portability at full value will increase dramatically. We are leaving behind a world in which the reputation of the college has been the major driver in the determined value of credited learning. Employers are increasingly dissatisfied with traditional college transcripts and the resumes to which they contribute, because neither accurately communicates the individual's true capacity. The C21C will connect its learning outcomes to both academic policies and program requirements and established workplace requirements, creating workplace-college articulation agreements that operate transparently.

Learners will use these direct agreements and equivalency measures to move their learning wherever and whenever they need to. They will be able to "shop" among various job opportunities as well as compare different learning options. They will become the "academic traffic controllers" of their own learning, using the C21C as their base of operations.

The adult-friendly C21C will exist as part of a far-flung web of interconnecting services, aligned by technology and consensus agreements, like the Bologna Process. These characteristics, taken collectively, will support and make possible a far more customized, personalized, and successful learning process.

As we have seen, timely degree completion with full recognition of credits earned is difficult for many of today's learners to achieve. The systems that are in place were largely structured for continuously enrolled, recent high school graduates. So, for the student who attends part time, comes and goes from semester to semester, and uses more than one institution's services, the barriers to credit recognition and transfer are significant and expensive in terms of time and money. A systemic, integrated solution is necessary if we are going to address comprehensively the barriers to academic credit portability that the majority of learners face, including those in the middle third.

AcademyOne, the credit transfer business, has designed and developed the Web site CollegeTransfer.net, an infrastructure to simplify academic credit portability. It is a remarkable example that portends the shape of things to come.

CollegeTransfer.net hosts tools and resources that institutions can use to evaluate and publish course equivalencies to the Web. The tools are designed to facilitate learners' transfer and articulation of college credit between institutions, while increasing transparency of the many pathways that lead to a degree. Over fifteen hundred postsecondary institutions' courses transfer to their client institutions, and nearly four thousand transfer and articulation agreements are included in their database.

AcademyOne offers a free, student-led service with each transfer profile page, which allows students to shop among institutions, comparing their offers for themselves. And the Web site now serves as the foundation for the Academic GPS, to help learners and their advisors navigate the continuum of higher education, which will touch learners at so many critical junctures in their lives. This model illustrates the type of service needed to enable learners to choose the institutions best suited to their needs.

Beginning as early as high school, a learner's transferable academic, career, and technical education experiences can be applied toward a postsecondary degree or credential. Throughout their lives, learners' job training, apprenticeships, and professional development experiences, as well as their personal learning, can be assessed and banked toward a postsecondary degree or credential.

Four services support learners and institutions.

- *Credential Consolidator.* This aggregates the entirety of a learner's postsecondary training into a standardized format, which includes coursework, college-level proficiency exams, corporate training, military experience and training, and applicable raw work and life experiences.

- *Credit Finder.* This helps learners equate postsecondary learning and their applicable experiences and credentials with evaluated college-level learning, such as standardized exams; credit recommendation services, such as the American Council on Education and the national Program on Noncollegiate Sponsored Instruction (PONSI); and the 3.5 million existing college-level courses in their up-to-date online course atlas.

- *Academic Evaluator.* This interprets a student's learning and translates it into a single, all-encompassing transcript, utilizing prior learning recognition methodologies.

- *Opportunity Locator.* This helps learners match their transcripts with degree and credential opportunities at a range of postsecondary institutions. It allows learners to compare opportunities, based on such factors as cost, time to completion, transferable credits, scheduling, and more (AcademyOne, 2008).

Armed with their Academic GPS, learners have the power to move their learning anywhere, anytime, seeking the best fit between their learning styles and existing programs. These services and the information they contain transform the academic landscape, giving the learner, as a comparison shopper, great power to choose the best academic fit according to their needs and requirements.

With this power comes a fundamental rebalancing of the relationship between the learner and college. Without an Academic GPS or its equivalent, the learner has been forced to approach each institution individually and accept the transfer terms without negotiation. With the GPS, learners can compare institutions on a real-time basis, making the best choices for themselves. As institutions, eager to enroll students, come to understand that they are losing qualified applicants based on this academic conceit, I believe the barriers to transfer, the "transfer tax" imposed when they require students to retake courses, will fall.

When the GPS system, or other models for credit portability, are linked directly to institutions ready to design and support learning opportunities that are comprehensive and adult friendly, one core element of the College of the Twenty-First Century will become a reality. The C21C recognizes, harnesses, and builds on learning, regardless of where or how it was acquired.

These five elements form the core of the College for the Twenty-First Century.

- Superb, end-to-end support services
- Consistent outcomes-based curricula, assessments, and course design
- Flexible degree architecture and programs of study
- Learning assessments that promote seamless transitions between life, work, and degree programs
- Global credit portability

Taken separately, each element can make a difference. Organized and aligned to support one another, these five elements can become the DNA of a new approach to learning support and recognition. This DNA will include accurate and current career information, helping adult learners plan and navigate their ways toward a degree while creating and incorporating career and personal pathways that guide and enrich their lives.

Institutions employing these elements will bridge the divide between classroom-based learning and learning that happens elsewhere. To be successful at bridging this divide, however, colleges will have to take additional, difficult steps. They need to recalibrate their relationships with the world around them, building in more learning-centric attitudes. In a world characterized by knowledge abundance, in which content is constructed collaboratively and learners can make many more decisions, the rules and hierarchies created by history's culture of scarcity no longer pertain. The assumptions governing the relationship between the lifelong learner and the College of the Twenty-First Century will change profoundly.

Colleges for the Twenty-First Century will also have to reinforce their underlying policies to recognize and develop the full implications and significance of these five elements. We have seen how portability is compromised by the refusal to accept the credit. And we know that even the best learning outcomes and assessments become hollow shells if employers and colleges don't keep them updated and agree to their handling and recognition.

Fueled by a new ecology of learning, the world of higher education and lifelong learning has been turned upside down. Charles Darwin argued that survival went to neither the strongest nor the smartest, but to those who could adapt the best to changing environments. Traditional colleges will struggle to adapt and survive in this radically changing world. We need them to succeed if America is going to have a chance at meeting its emerging civic, social, and workforce requirements.

The secret to continued, broader societal and economic success, driven by more opportunities in higher education, however, lies outside of those institutions. Instead, it dwells in new designs for learning, which build on the elements of the new ecology of learning. It is there that we will harness America's wasted talent.

Conclusion: A New Ecology of Learning

The Merriam-Webster Online Dictionary defines ecology as "the pattern of relations between organisms and their environment." The myriad forces, new tools, and knowledge populating the learning landscape have created an emerging new ecology of learning in America. It is as real as the "pattern of relations" that make up a bubbling brook or a beautiful estuary where marine life abounds. And, just as climate has changed over the years, affecting different regions of the world in different ways, this new ecology reflects a change in the ways we can support, recognize, and employ learning, which is fundamentally different from the traditional ecology of higher education represented in the organization of our campuses.

It is important to understand that the new ecology of learning will change forever the balance of power between the learner and his or her learning, where it happens, how it happens, and how it is recognized and valued. Learners can now, with very little effort, pick and choose among dozens of institutions by comparison shopping for programs that suit them. They can also compare the time to obtain a degree and resulting cost of completing their education, which varies according to differing treatments of their transfer credits and their abilities to continue working while studying.

In this new ecology, adult learners are transformed from powerless petitioners to careful consumers in their relationships with colleges and universities, shopping for the degrees and the learning policies that best align with their circumstances and needs.

Imagine Peace Corps volunteers, or Teach for America recruits, using the training they receive and the experience they have as active elements in their lifelong education. The volunteer might access a water systems engineering site to learn more about how to build a better water system in a rural Honduran village. Or the recruit might access a learning style inventory to understand better the learners in front of him or her. Or, beyond that, the recruit might use the eLab now offered online by MIT to promote science studies that were impossible in earlier days. All of this activity can now be understood, recognized, and packaged as learning.

The new ecology of learning has three core elements that support the personalization, customization, and portability of learning services. Together, they create a new balance of power that supports and encourages the potential for high-quality learning anywhere, anytime.

First, when it comes to knowledge, information, and access, the era of scarcity has ended. We face a future of abundance, in terms of not only content but also access to and manipulation of that content. This radical shift in the sheer volume of high-quality and diverse content, as well as unfettered access to it, permanently changes the relationship between the individual, his or her own learning and education, and the institution called college.

Second, the technology we are developing will, in addition to ending scarcity, create previously unimaginable variety, quality, and consistency in educational delivery and support services. The barriers that protected the one-size-fits-all approach to teaching and learning have been permanently breached. With the fall of these barriers comes a new relationship between the individual learner and the means by which he or she learns.

Finally, embedded in these two new realities is the ability to adapt educational services to the needs of the learner—taking into account how people learn, why they learn, and what they want to learn. Customization of services and personalization of relation-ships with each learner will tap the talent of many more people who are ready to learn and fully capable of doing so.

Learning's emerging new ecology reflects a profound change in relationships among learners, their learning, the workplace, and the institutions that support them. Colleges and universities used to control the conversation and the flow of learning, making the rules that dictated the enterprise and its boundaries with the remainder of the world. In that old ecology, it was largely incon-ceivable that learners, as a matter of course, might shop among colleges, comparing acceptance of transfer credit earned elsewhere; outcomes-based programs versus more traditional, input-oriented programs; or online learning instead of a day or weekend, place-based approach. Even more unlikely was the design control that learners will be able to exercise in the future over the learning they pursue.

It all comes down to this as we rethink college for the twenty-first century. There is only one person for whom learning, educa-tion, and life happen up close and personal: the learner. Learning happens in a continuing stream, for each of us. And the great gift that the new ecology of learning gives us is to personalize and direct learning to each person's interests, strengths, and needs. Learner-centered design is no longer a gift we give to the learner. It is an environment that the learner can initiate and develop as the central actor in his or her own personal drama.

Talent does not have a name. Talent does not have an address. And talent does not have a face. Like the effervescence of fine champagne, talent will bubble up. As we rethink higher education, we will organize around talent, providing an expanding array of cups into which it can be poured.

Resources

Publications

Adelman, C. (1999). *Answers in the toolbox*. Washington, DC: USDOE.

Altbach, P. G., Berdahl, R. O., & Gumport, P. J. (Eds.). (1998). *American higher education in the twenty-first century*. Baltimore, MD: Johns Hopkins University Press.

American Association of Colleges and Universities (AAC&U). (2007). *College learning for the new global century*. Washington, DC: Author.

American College of Testing (ACT). (2006). *Ready for college and ready for work: Same or different?* Iowa City: Author.

Belenky, M. F., Clinchy, B. M., Goldberger, N. R., & Tarule, J. M. (1997). *Women's ways of knowing*. New York: Basic Books.

Britt, W. (2007). *ProSeminar briefing paper*. Fort Lauderdale, FL: Kaplan University, Student Services.

Cairncross, F. (1997). *The death of distance: How the communications revolution will change our lives*. Cambridge, MA: Harvard Business School Press.

Carnevale, A. P., & Fry, R. A. (2002). The demographic window of opportunity. In D. Heller (Ed.), *Condition of access: Higher Education for lower income students*. Westport, CT: American Council on Education and Praeger Studies.

Christiansen, C. (1997). *The innovator's dilemma.* Cambridge, MA: Harvard Business School Press.

Baum, S., & Payea, K. (2007). *Education pays: The benefits of higher education for individuals and society.* Princeton, NJ: The College Board.

Collins, J. (2001). *Good to great: Why some companies make the leap ... and others don't.* New York: Harper Collins.

Council of Adult Experiential Learning (CAEL). (2008). *State policies to bring adult learning in focus.* Chicago: Author.

Council on Competitiveness. (2008). *Thrive: The skills imperative.* Washington, DC: Author.

Flint, T. A., & Associates. (1999). *Best practices in adult learning: A CAEL/ APQD benchmarking study.* New York: Forbes Custom.

Guilford, J. P. (1967). *The nature of human intelligence.* New York: McGraw-Hill.

Holzer, H., & Lerman, R. (2007). *America's forgotten middle-skill jobs: Education and training requirements in the next decade and beyond.* Washington, DC.: Georgetown University, Skills2Compete/Urban Institute.

Lorenz, M. (2007). *Degree plan universalization.* Chicago: Kaplan University, Registrar's Office.

National Commission on Adult Literacy. (2008). *Reach higher, America: Overcoming crisis in the U.S. workforce.* Washington, DC: Author.

Ouellette, B. (2008). *Learning recognition and portability.* Fort Lauderdale, FL: Kaplan Higher Education.

Partnership for 21st Century Skills. (2008). *21st century skills, education, and competitiveness.* Tucson, AZ: Author.

Senge, P. (1990). *The fifth discipline: The art and practice of the learning organization.* New York: Currency.

Society for Human Resource Management (SHRM). (2008). *Workforce forecast.* Alexandria, VA: Author.

State Higher Education Executive Officers (SHEEO). (2009). *The college degree gap.* Boulder, CO: Author.

U.S. Census Bureau. (2007). *Current population survey: Education attainment of the population 18 and over.* Washington, DC.

U.S. Department of Labor. (2008). *America's dynamic workforce.* Washington, DC.

Western Interstate Commission for Higher Education (WICHE). (2008). *Knocking on the college door: Projections of high school graduates.* Boulder, CO: Author.

Web sites

www.americancollegeoftesting.org

www.open.ac.uk

www.rethinkinghighereducation.com

www.thetechnium.com

References

AcademyOne. (2008). *An academic GPS*. Philadelphia: Author.

Anderson, C. (2006). *The long tail*. New York: Hyperion.

Bloom, B. S., & Krathwohl, D. R. (1956). *Taxonomy of educational objectives: The classification of educational goals, by a committee of college and university examiners. Handbook 1: Cognitive domain*. New York: Longman.

Brock, W. E. (2001, Sept.). *Focus on each child*. Paper presented at the Education Leaders Council, Phoenix, AZ.

Bureau of Labor Statistics (BLS). (2008). Office of Occupational Statistics and Employment Practices. Washington, DC: Author.

Burn, B. B. (2002). *Expanding the international dimension of higher education*. (Business-Higher Education Forum). Washington, DC: American Council on Education.

Carey, K. (2009, Apr. 3). What colleges should learn from newspapers' decline. *Chronicle of Higher Education*.

Christiansen, C. (2008). *Disrupting class*. New York: McGraw-Hill.

Dewey, J. (1916). *Democracy and education*. New York: MacMillan.

Gardner, H. (1983). *Frames of mind: The theory of multiple intelligences*. New York: Basic Books.

General Accounting Office (GAO). (2005). *Transfer students: Postsecondary institutions could promote more consistent consideration of coursework by not basing determinations on accreditation.* Washington, DC: Author.

Gladwell, M. (2000). *The tipping point: How little things make a big difference.* New York: Little, Brown.

Gross, B., & Goldhaber, D. (2009). *Community college transfer and articulation policies: Looking beneath the surface.* Seattle, WA: Center on Reinventing Public Education.

Guilford, J. P. (1956). The structure of intellect. *Psychological Bulletin, 52,* 267–293.

Illich, I. (1971). *Deschooling society.* San Francisco: Harper & Row.

Ittelson, J. (2008, Summer). Know your ePortfolio. *Converge,* 32–35.

Jones, R. (2009). *The new American workforce: Challenges and opportunities for higher education.* Washington, DC: Springboard Project, Business Round Table.

Keller, G. (1983). *Academic strategy.* Baltimore: Johns Hopkins University Press.

Kuhn, T. S. (1962). *The structure of scientific revolutions.* Chicago: University of Chicago Press.

Lewin, T. (2008, Dec. 3). Higher education may soon be unaffordable for most Americans. *New York Times.*

Massachusetts Institute of Technology/Open CourseWare Project (MIT/OCW). (2008). Board report. CourseWare Project.

Means, B., et al. (2009). *Evaluation of evidence-based practices in online learning.* Washington, DC: United States Department of Education, Center for Technology in Learning.

Meeker, M. (1969). *The structure of intellect: Its uses and interpretations.* Columbus, OH: Charles Merrill.

Mortenson, T. (2002). *ACT institutional survey, NCES-IPEDS graduation rate survey*. Boulder, CO: National Center for Higher Education Management Systems.

National Center for Public Policy and Higher Education (NCPPHE). (2008). *Measuring up, 2008: National report card on higher education*. San Jose: Author.

Porter, M. (2008, Oct. 30). Why America needs an economic strategy. *BusinessWeek*.

Sanders, S. (2008). *General education proposal*. Fort Lauderdale, FL: Kaplan University.

Scheckley, B. G., & Keeton, M. T. (2001). *Improving employee development: Perspectives from research and practice*. Chicago: Council for Adult and Experiential Learning.

Sheehy, G. (1976). *Passages*. New York: E. P. Dutton.

Smith, P. (1986). *Your hidden credentials: The value of learning outside of college*. Washington, DC: Acropolis Books.

Smith, P. (2004). *The quiet crisis: How higher education is failing America*. San Francisco: Jossey-Bass.

Stegner, W. (1971). *Angle of repose*. Doubleday. New York.

Structure of Intellect Systems (SOI). (1982). *Relationship of Structure of Intellect (SOI) abilities to school curriculum programming*. Vida, OR: Author.

Tough, A. (1971). *The adult's learning projects: A fresh approach to theory and practice in adult learning*. Ontario Institute for Studies in Education of the University of Toronto.

United States Department of Education, National Center for Education Statistics. (2001). *Digest of education statistics 2001*. Washington, DC: USDoE.

Wallis, C. (2008, Nov. 26). Bill and Melinda Gates go back to school, *Fortune*.

Wiggins, G., & McTighe, J. (2005). *Understanding by design*. Alexandria, VA: ASCD.

Index

and, 84, 86; historical actions
in, xx, 24; remoteness of, 15
Financial institutions, 19
Flexibility: of C21Cs, 145–148; of
technology, 126–128
Foreign policy, 9
Frames of Mind (Gardner), 59
Franklin, B., 101, 124
Freshman seminars, 61
Frontal lobe, of brain, x
Future, of America, 4–5

G

Gardner, H., 45, 56, 59–61, 62,
64, 65
Gates Foundation, 50, 54, 87
General Accounting Office,
84–85
General education, 130
George Washington University,
xxi
GI Bill, xx, 23, 48, 52, 98, 100,
135
Gladwell, M., 114
Global economy, 9, 16, 19
Global workforce, 19
Goal setting, 56, 57
Goldhaber, D., 82
Government, American, 7, 9
Graduate students, 125
Graduation: of C21C programs,
145–148; in current educational
models, xvi; economic effects
of, 11; hidden costs of, 50; job
growth and, 16; online learning
advantages and, 131; rates of,
xiii, 16; reasons for decrease in,
35, 110–112; time wasted to
achieve, 44; transfer costs of,
86; transfer restrictions and, 81,
82–83, 84

Gross, B., 82
Guilford, J. P., 63

H

Harvard Graduate School of
Education, 58
Head Start training courses, xi
Hewlett Foundation, 124
Higher education: angle of
repose in, 4–5; barriers to,
67–68, 74–77, 95–96, 104;
cottage-industry nature of, 21;
dangerous assumptions of, 1;
decreased opportunity because
of, 37; denying access to, 16;
diminishing returns in, 29–34;
diversity of, 21, 22; division of
personal versus academic
learning in, 20; economic
effects of failure of, 10; failure
toward minority populations
of, 28–29; historical structure
and purpose of, 54–55;
increased access to, 29, 38,
47–48; ineffective cost control
of, 26–27, 30; international
respect for, 10; lack of
technology adoption by, 26,
107–112; location of, 95–96,
104–105; maxed-out nature of,
27–34; new ecology of
learning and, 157–158;
number of colleges in, 21,
23–24; physical capacity of,
110–112; power of, 159;
prestige of, 97; remoteness of,
14–15, 67–68; resistance to
change in, 24–26, 33, 53; size
of colleges in, 25; strengths of,
21–22; students' failure to
thrive in, 51–52; success